ADVANCE PRAISE FOR *PLANETARY CITIZENSHIP*

"The interaction of these two brilliant minds have brought out won-derful ideas, thoughts and analyses on issues of relevance to the present and future generations. Their empathy for humanity is eloquently expressed, providing great intellectual stimulation to any reader."
— **Anwarul K. Chowdhury, under-secretary-general**
of the United Nations

"This book is full of gems of wisdom from both the authors on both the moral al import of applying their values to the real life problems that confront all of human kind."
— **Richard L. Ottinger, dean emeritus,**
Pace Law School, New York

"A feast for the heart, soul and mind! Henderson and Ikeda serve up tasty portions of wisdom gleaned from decades of global activism. Sit back and savor *Planetary Citizenship*, then celebrate by using these fresh insights to enhance your own recipes for a joyful, values-based life."
— **Hal Brill, author,** *Investing with Your Values:*
Making Money and Making a Difference

"This book carries a clear and urgent message for our planet — our earth needs you! It paints a clear vision of how ordinary people have achieved extraordinary things in working to safeguard the future of us all."
— **Annabel McGoldrick, peace journalist, author, co-director,**
Reporting the World, Oxford, United Kingdom

"This dialogue between two giants of the naturalistic philosophy that informs concrete action toward achieving equitable, sustainable development is not to be missed by anyone involved in the subject."
— **Daniel M. Smith, colonel, USA (ret.), senior fellow**
for military affairs, Friends Committee on
National Legislation, Washington, D.C.

"An insightful and lively dialogue on the intellectual and political initiatives toward a more human and environmentally responsible future by two important leaders in the field."
— **Sander G. Tideman, chair, Spirit in Business, Bussum, The Netherlands**

"Henderson and Ikeda, two of the world's foremost thinkers and applied visionaries, show us how we can transform crisis into opportunity and inspire us with their examples."
— **Rodger Spiller, Ph.D., CFP, Socially Responsible Investment specialist, Auckland, New Zealand**

"Promoting a philosophy of health and happiness based on an economy of caring and sharing, Drs. Henderson and Ikeda foresee a future that reveals our greatest potential. Their wisdom reflects the old proverb, 'He who has health has hope and he who has hope has everything.'"
— **Ellen Taliaferro, M.D., executive director, Pandora Project, California, United States of America**

"To be really effective, a policy of environmental sustainability must be anchored in the minds and hearts of people, of ordinary people, not just in politicians and other high-level decision makers. This book is a great contribution."
— **Bedrich Moldan, director, Environment Centre, Charles University, Czech Republic**

"An important contribution to the urgent task of re-engineering the DNA of global capitalism. This excellent book rightly draws our attention to the root cause — and some creative solutions — to our challenge: intellectual and institutional inertia."
— **Matthew Kiernan, chief executive, Innovest Strategic Value Advisors, Toronto, Canada**

Planetary
Citizenship

Your Values, Beliefs, and Actions
Can Shape a Sustainable World

Planetary
Citizenship

Your Values, Beliefs, and Actions
Can Shape a Sustainable World

HAZEL HENDERSON
AND DAISAKU IKEDA

MIDDLEWAY
PRESS

Editor's note: This book was originally published in Japan in *Ushio* magazine (2002). It was later published in book form on January 2, 2003. For this English-language edition, working closely with the authors, we rearranged, revised and updated the text of the Japanese edition. We trust this edited version accurately conveys the authors' intentions.

Originally published as *Chikyu taidan kagayaku josei no seiki he* by Shufu no Tomo Sha (publisher), Tokyo.

Published by Middleway Press
A division of the SGI-USA
606 Wilshire Blvd., Santa Monica, CA 90401

ISBN 0-9723267-2-3

Cover and interior design by Lightbourne, Inc.
Cover photo www.gettyimages.com

10 9 8 7 6 5 4 3 2 1

Library of Congress Cataloging-in-Publication Data

Henderson, Hazel, 1933-
  Planetary citizenship : your values, beliefs and actions can shape a sustainable future / Hazel Henderson and Daisaku Ikeda.
      p. cm.
  Includes index.
  ISBN 0-9723267-2-3 (hardcover : alk. paper)
  1. Environmentalism. 2. Sustainable development — Citizen participation.
I. Ikeda, Daisaku. II. Title.
  GE195.H46 2004
  333.72 — dc22
                              200400674

CONTENTS

TO THE ENGLISH EDITION

I WELCOME NEW READERS to this English translation of my dialogue with Daisaku Ikeda from its original Japanese edition. We have added some thoughts relevant to global issues that have developed since our dialogue. The concepts of planetary citizenship and evolving personal responsibility for our human future are now clear. Indeed, many are calling this worldwide emergence of grassroots people's movements the newest global superpower. Yet it is composed of ordinary people just like you and me.

I remember an early morning in 1961, watching the sunrise over the towers of midtown Manhattan. I was nursing my three-month-old baby. Like many New Yorkers that morning, I witnessed on television as astronaut Alan Shepard blasted off on his first flight into space. In amazement, I murmured to my busy daughter, "You are a space-age baby!"

Today we are all space-age humans. We ponder this new stage in our evolution as we view the wondrous photographs of our home taken from the moon. This extraordinary image of our luminous blue and white planet floating in the blackness of space is now in the mindscape of most of the six billion members of our human family.

At the school in the small English village where I grew up, our teacher taught her geography classes by proudly showing us a world map dominated by pink areas depicting the British Empire. Since then, many empires have fallen along with Britain's. Today's children learn about humanity's two hundred or so nation-states in a world dominated by globe-girdling technologies, all jostling for military or economic advantage over one another and over nature's diminishing resources.

As humans spread from our beginnings in Africa to every continent on earth, we have inherited all the long, painful strivings of our ancestors. We are part of the 4.5-billion-year unfolding of life on this planet. What will be the next step in our evolution? The great religions and traditions of our human family have reflected our struggles to understand our past and guide our present behavior and our steps into the future. All contain a core of shared wisdom — the Golden Rule to treat others as we wish to be treated — and each of us carries within us a spark of the divine, the infinite, the universal.

Of all these human wisdom traditions, which teachings can best lead us toward a future of peace, justice and harmony with all life? Which beliefs have proved dysfunctional and need to be discarded as we proceed on our journey, now as a planetary and interplanetary species? A dear and thoughtful friend, Virginia Straus, facilitates such vital dialogues at the Boston Research Center for the 21st Century, founded by Daisaku Ikeda. Recently, Virginia introduced me to Ira Rifkin, whose book *Spiritual Perspectives on Globalization* describes how major human faith traditions are addressing one of the main issues of our time: globalization and its current economic and technological forms.

Peace and nonviolence are now widely identified as fundamental to human survival. Competition must be balanced by cooperation and sharing. Even economists agree that peace, nonviolence and human security are global public goods along with clean air and water, health and education — bedrock conditions for human well-being and development. As Daisaku Ikeda and I discuss, however, we must remember that economics is not a science and its current dominance over nations' policies must give way to more multidisciplinary approaches. We discuss the shortcomings of measuring human progress by the growth of our "economies" rather than the larger social context of improving quality of life for all.

As human technologies evolved — global communications, satellites, weapons of mass destruction and distraction — questions reemerge about the makeup of human nature. Are we simply "naked apes," a mammalian species colonizing every niche on planet earth, devouring 40 percent of all primary photosynthesis production of its biosphere, driving other species to another Great Extinction?

Daisaku Ikeda and I believe that we ourselves are evolving into wider awareness of our responsibilities as planetary citizens. Will our godlike collective technological powers drive us either toward destruction or toward redesigning our societies, cultures and values to reflect our new place in nature? These questions are at the heart of our dialogue in this book, which focuses on the way our personal values, goals and beliefs can work in our families and communities toward a more sustainable future for all.

These new debates are already defining this twenty-first century. It is evident that the "hare" of technological innovation has outrun the "tortoise" of social innovation. This lag underlies all today's global issues, from how to control weapons of mass destruction, human cloning, genetically modified foods, agriculture and basic materials (via nanotechnology) to health, new epidemics, education, the role of global mass media for good and ill, environmental degradation, pollution and climate change.

Underlying all these issues is that of how to steer technological powers toward genuine human development, sustainable prosperity and social progress. Ever since the founding of the United Nations in 1945 "to free humanity from the scourge of war" and the Universal Declaration of Human Rights, humans have been quietly hammering out these issues underlying our global future.

Daisaku Ikeda's many initiatives to strengthen and revitalize the United Nations predate my own and have contributed to my understanding. The United Nations has fostered many global agreements that have led to enforceable treaties and international law covering arms control, health, environmental protection and exchange of scientific knowledge. Many of these have been spurred on by grassroots movements and the burgeoning of civil society as a new force in world. The largest mass demonstrations ever (estimated at between ten and fifteen million people) in cities around the world against the war on Iraq revealed this new "third force" of planetary citizens.

The influence of planetary citizens lies beyond national boundaries and requires new forms of global representation, such as the people's assembly being advocated at the United Nations. This upwelling of planetary citizenship includes the Earth Charter (www.earthcharter.org), the Parliament of the World's Religions, Forum 2000 and the Prague Declaration launched by former Czech President Václav Havel, the Hague Appeal for Peace, the arms control and children's rights campaigns of Nobel Prize winners Oscar Arias Sánchez, Betty Williams, Jody Williams and Nelson Mandela and Mother Teresa's work for the poor and sick. We can even include Princess Diana's short-lived humanitarian efforts; her death led to a global outpouring of grief as some 2 billion people — one-third of the planet's inhabitants — watched her funeral on television.

People everywhere have begun to understand the "CNN effect" and are focusing on the unfulfilled power of communications technologies for good. Today, we all live in media-ocracies, whether our older government structures are democratic, feudal, authoritarian or fascist. Mass media are the nervous systems of our body politic wherever we live. We the people have learned about current media bias and spin and that whoever controls mass communications wins elections, power, money, fame and influence. Internet-based platforms now globally link media reformers and planetary citizens. Their movements for peace, health, education, environment and visionary projects demonstrate human courage, responsibility and potential to shape positive directions for our global future.

Mass media can either be a positive force in these efforts or can continue to enmesh humanity in negative images of primitive and violent behavior and cycles of revenge. Many journalists already accept the new media responsibilities. The new journalism and media are already digging deeper for the causes of today's violent events. They will devote equal time to the unreported positive stories of community development, local leadership, individual entrepreneurship and social innovation to inspire billions of humans toward new possibilities for a brighter future.

My concerns about all of these issues have led to many visits to Brazil, a new beacon of hope for democracy. Brazil gave birth to the World Social Forum, the leading virtual organization of global citizens and Civil Society Organizations framing viable alternatives to the now-discredited "Washington Consensus" model of GNP growth (laissez-faire "free" markets and trade, privatizations, export-led economies dominated by the globalization of unregulated finance leading to currency speculation).

Brazil has staked out many new directions and social innovations described in my editorials "Brazil: Key Player in a New World Game," "Visioning Brazil 2020" and "Statisticians of the World Unite!" (www.hazelhenderson.com).

In October 2003, I was proud to be involved in bringing together seven hundred quality-of-life and sustainable development statisticians from all over Latin America, Europe, Asia and North America to compare notes on multidisciplinary approaches to redefining wealth and progress. For example, Bhutan's new indicators of Gross National Happiness, reflecting the goals of this Buddhist nation, exemplify the importance of clarifying the goals and values of a society and creating indicators to measure what we treasure: health, happiness, education, human rights, family, country, harmony, peace and environmental quality and restoration.

Daisaku Ikeda and I discuss all these issues in our dialogue, including our passionate support of grassroots efforts to promote the goals and aspirations of ordinary people everywhere. North, South, East and West — polls conducted (by Globescan in the United Kingdom) in more than sixty countries show that these are the priorities of the people, yet too many governments spend precious taxes on weapons, conflict and the technology agendas of military contractors and global corporations.

Despite many frustrations with entrenched power elites, the Information Age is slowly morphing into a new Age of Truth. Corporate fraud and accounting scandals, bribery and government corruption can no longer be hidden. When civic activists highlight irresponsible company behavior, corporate brand names can be damaged. For example, corporations that signed on in 1999 to the UN Global Compact and its nine principles of good corporate citizenship are now being held accountable by ethical auditing firms and citizen watchdog groups.

From sunny Porto Alegre, Brazil, came the World Social Forum's challenge to snowy Davos, Switzerland, and its World Economic Forum: "Another World is Possible." Many visions and viable programs for an equitable, ecologically sustainable future come from people's deepest spiritual understandings. Every faith tradition can contribute together with the deep sense of responsibility of millions who act from personal compassion. We share the conviction that human beings will continue to evolve toward the ethics so well stated in the Earth Charter, which we discuss at length in this book.

I hope you enjoy this dialogue as much as Daisaku Ikeda and I did, and that you may find our conversations a spur within your own circles. I also hope you will send me your ideas, which can be posted on a Web site I have helped to launch, VIA3 ("Third Way" in Latin), based in London. Please visit me there at www.via3.net.

Hazel Henderson
St. Augustine, Florida
May 2004

ONE

A Life of Civic Action

DAISAKU IKEDA • Desires have been the driving force behind the development of modern civilization. We have made nature and life itself means to an end. As you, Hazel Henderson — a civic activist and writer working to expand global citizens' movements — frequently point out, traditional economics has abetted the process. But now, at the beginning of the twenty-first century, we have reached our limits. The selfish pursuit of happiness has boomeranged, leading to the sufferings resulting from biotechnological and environmental problems and to the proliferation of weapons of mass destruction.

Any lasting global solutions to these challenges must begin with what we might call individual human revolution. This means that instead of being absorbed in the minor self of the ego, each individual must recognize his or her connection with all life in the cosmos. By doing so, we can escape our obsession with greed, advance along a more compassionate path, and bring about mutual happiness for ourselves and others. I am certain that this is the key to creating a new civilization founded on the dignity of life.

I am extremely happy to conduct this dialogue with you. Our themes, planetary citizenship and the future of humanity, give us a broad scope for discussion.

HAZEL HENDERSON • I am delighted at the chance to engage in discussions with you because, in addition to having a splendid vision, you have consistently worked with hope and optimism to make the world a better place.

The world has many problems. But if we pool our strengths and confront them, we are certain to find ways to solve them. Crises and problems give us the chance to create a better future.

Home as the starting point

IKEDA • We human beings have created our problems, and I am confident we can solve them. As you say, we face a mountain of difficulties — war and violence, oppression and poverty, environmental destruction and so on. We must make the twenty-first century an age in which human beings resolve their problems by first reforming themselves.

The need for inner reform is nowhere more obvious than in the terrorist attacks against the United States on September 11, 2001. Inevitably arousing wrath, terrorist acts represent the ultimate in inhumanity because of the indifference with which they destroy the precious lives of many people. They are an absolute evil that cannot be justified by any cause, no matter how great.

HENDERSON • I was deeply shocked by the attacks on New York and Washington. Terrorists must be faced and checked, and such criminals who act against humanity must be brought to justice. At the same time, we must avoid knee-jerk military strikes. Eye-for-an-eye dogmas belong to history, not to the twenty-first century. Just after the attacks, I wrote in my syndicated column that we must seek a solution that does not invite further terrorist violence and the sacrifice of more poverty-stricken innocents. I advocated the convening of a terrorism summit, in which the United Nations must play the leading role

2

since it is the only organization with a big enough tent to accommodate all countries.[1]

IKEDA • Although it is a difficult issue, I believe that how we deal with the absolute evil of terrorism and the chain of hatred and violence will provide the touchstone that defines the development of the twenty-first century.

The United Nations convened intensive debates on terrorism for more than five days starting on October 1, 2001. For the first time, UN discussions were restricted to one topic. Representatives of 167 nations addressed the meetings, which reemphasized the importance of the United Nations as a place for dialogues. I believe that down-to-earth, intercivilizational dialogues that embrace the spiritual dimension, the coming together of those who believe in the good of human nature and wish to make a difference, should be held on terrorism and many other problems.

We all live on the same planet. We must therefore employ dialogue to deepen mutual understanding and to redirect the vector of history from confrontation to peaceful coexistence and from isolation to solidarity.

HENDERSON • That is very true. Just as happened in the 1930s, today's current economic and technological globalization could collapse in another worldwide recession and prolonged war. To prevent this, we must help shape a more just and ecologically sustainable global economy. Doing so would promote peace and security as well.

Economic competition has been ruled by the law of the jungle. Unless we balance this with cooperation, we face a lose–lose situation. Many scholars and millions of concerned people are now leading and showing how we must change our ways. On our small, endangered planet, we must make human society a win–win situation of peace and harmonious coexistence.

IKEDA • It is vital, then, that we transcend differences in interests and national boundaries and see just how far we can expand the global solidarity of peoples.

For many years, you have been a leader in environmental and civic movements. As we talk about your experiences, I should like to try to discover the optimum path for humanity to pursue.

But first I propose that we spend some time talking about your earlier life and mine. Our dialogue, I believe, will be more fruitful if we deepen our mutual understanding by learning about each other's background.

HENDERSON • I agree.

Two seaside towns

IKEDA • To start, then, I was born in the Omori district of Tokyo in January 1928. Though now densely built up with houses and factories, in my childhood, Omori was a relaxed seaside village dotted with the homes of families who processed edible seaweeds.

HENDERSON • I have heard that Omori seaweed products were considered among the best.

IKEDA • You are well informed. Tell me about your hometown.

HENDERSON • I was born in southwestern England in the city of Bristol in 1933. When I was five, we moved to a suburb called Clevedon, which, like your birthplace, is on the sea. We had a lot of seaweed in Clevedon, but English people didn't know what to do with it. We didn't know it was good to eat. It was only when I went to Japan that I found out.

Clevedon is a small village with a population of about three thousand, but men of letters and poets have long loved its beautiful natural setting. Tennyson, Thackeray and Coleridge are known to have lived there for a while.

IKEDA • Some of Tennyson's poems concern the sea. Perhaps its beauty attracted him to Clevedon.

The Omori sea, too, was beautiful when I was a child. Fields of seasonally blooming flowers and wave-lapped beaches provided perfect playgrounds for a boy like me.

Unfortunately, the sea there is now polluted, and much of the shore is reclaimed land. The traditional raising of edible seaweed there, which had dated back to the seventeenth and eighteenth centuries, was abandoned about forty years ago. I wish children in urban areas today had more chances to appreciate the beauty of the natural environment.

HENDERSON • It's hard to watch your hometown's natural environment destroyed. I now live in Florida, but I remember going back to Clevedon a few years ago and walking down the main street. It looked just the same as when I was a child — at least the parts you could see. But in the parts you couldn't see, in the water and soil, pollution was spreading.

IKEDA • How, exactly?

HENDERSON • To give a simple example, you can no longer eat the fish caught off Clevedon. My mother used to take us every morning to buy fish from people fishing off a local pier. It was fresh, and she'd cook it in different ways for us. Today you can't eat that fish. It's dangerously full of cadmium from a nearby factory. All over the world, in their single-minded pursuit of profit, people sacrifice the environment and overlook the loss incurred through pollution. For many years, I have been advocating a shift from this environmentally destructive economic policy. A trip back to Clevedon reinforced my conviction.

Silent Spring

IKEDA • Taken by themselves, the case of the seaweed or the fish may seem trivial; but, added up, all such instances of pollution may result in an irreversible situation. The biologist Rachel Carson, in her famous book *Silent Spring*, was one of the earliest to warn of this danger. The writer Sawako Ariyoshi introduced Rachel Carson's ideas in her own widely read work, *Fukugo Osen* (Compound Pollution).

HENDERSON • When it was published in 1962, *Silent Spring* aroused a furor in America. Carson laid bare the influences that agricultural chemicals and fertilizers were exerting on nature and humanity. She was vilified and ridiculed by reductionist scientists and hounded by angry chemical corporations. But she didn't give in. Later the government said she was right and prohibited dangerous agricultural chemicals. Her voice brought down a thick wall.

I first read the book in 1964, when I was living in New York and about to start a big movement to stop atmospheric pollution. Carson lived in Pittsburgh, one of the most polluted U.S. cities, where steel mills vomited out smoke everywhere. Her struggle was one of the things that encouraged me to take a stand.

IKEDA • Both you and Rachel Carson insist on the urgent need to break with the profit-first social structure that ignores ecology. This idea, that we must establish political and economic goals fundamentally based on life values, is what inspired me to call the twenty-first century the Century of Life.

HENDERSON • The vision behind the Century of Life agrees with my Politics of the Solar Age and a new Age of Light and Enlightenment, in which all individuals must reexamine their beliefs and values, expanding their horizons to see our true situation. With this knowledge, they can challenge obsolete authority figures.

From childhood, my parents instilled in me the attitude to question everything, not just blindly accept what I was told. Accordingly, I always questioned authority. I always stopped and thought for myself before making judgments. I didn't realize then what a gift that was! I'm very grateful to them now.

Parents

IKEDA • What a fine attitude. You are fortunate to have had such excellent parents.

HENDERSON • My father was an accountant at a pulp and cardboard factory in Bristol. A rather typical father of the time — a little despotic and stubborn, he was often absent because of work. Really, my mother was the anchor of my life and taught me how to love and learn. I was the second daughter and had one older sister and two younger brothers. Mother was a very loving person. She did lots of volunteer work at the local baby clinic and provided meals for elderly shut-ins. She taught me the importance of loving people and how to think about things.

What kind of people were your parents?

IKEDA • My father was stubborn enough to be called Mr. Hardhead by our neighbors. He was a good man, a persevering and patient man whose obstinacy was backed by absolute honesty. My mother, cheerful and kind, was always working, either doing household chores or helping in the family business.

When I was in elementary school, my father was confined to a sickbed for two years. Mother became our mainstay, working as hard as she could to bring all her children up lovingly.

I learned a lot from my parents. My father taught me the importance of living by one's convictions; my mother taught me a cheerful attitude and to persevere, no matter how hard things got.

Children of World War II

IKEDA • We share the experience of having spent the most impressionable time of our lives under wartime conditions. As Mikhail Gorbachev said to me once, ours might justly be called the generation of war children, epitomized by the hardships and privations we experienced.

The year after I was born came the Great Depression, a contributive factor in the outbreak of World War II. Before the wounds of World War I had healed, the world was once again about to be plunged into the quagmire of all-out combat.

In Japan, with each passing day, the tramp of military boots grew louder. One by one, my older brothers were called up. Militarism was drilled into our young heads even in elementary school. First came the invasion of China, then the attack on Pearl Harbor in 1941, when we were plunged into total war. I was thirteen.

HENDERSON • So we share memories of the tempest of war. I suffered few hardships during the war because my mother always protected us. Making sure we had food to eat was her biggest worry. We were on very tight rations: two ounces of butter per person each week, two ounces of meat and two ounces of sugar. We had our own hens, and my mother grew all our own food. She was a wonderful gardener, and we bought fish for extra protein. And if we had known seaweed was good to eat, our diet would have been a little richer.

IKEDA • Of course, diets are different in different cultures.

My mother, too, had a lot of children to feed. We had one hen. Each egg it laid went to a child, in order of seniority. Since there were so many of us, the youngest rarely got one. One morning, I remember, my younger brother went to the chicken house and came back clapping his hands and shouting that the hen had produced four eggs! We later found out that mother had gotten up early, gone out to buy eggs, and put them in the chicken coop for us.

Incidentally, can you remember anything from the start of World War II?

HENDERSON • I was only six. England declared war on Germany when the Nazis invaded Poland in September 1939. I remember when the news was broadcast. My parents and many uncles and aunts were in a room in my grandmother's house, sitting around the radio. To my amazement, everybody was crying. I wondered what was going to happen.

Nothing more barbarous, nothing more cruel

IKEDA • I was thirteen when Japan went to war with the United States in December 1941. My memories of it are still as fresh as the day it happened. To help the family make ends meet, my older brother and I delivered the newspapers that told of what was happening. Even as small children, we could sense unusual tension, even excitement.

Then, as Japan's defeat drew near in 1945, the Americans intensified their air raids. To keep fire from spreading, the house we had lived in for so many years was razed. The whole family planned to take refuge in an aunt's house. Little by little, we loaded our belongings onto a bicycle-drawn cart. It took hours and was hard on a tuberculosis sufferer like me. Then, on the night before we were to move, a direct hit burned our aunt's house down. As incendiary bombs set the neighborhood aflame, my younger brother and I dashed about saving what little we could from our luggage. I still remember how frightened I was.

We managed to drag out only one trunk, and it turned out to be the one filled with a set of dolls for the early spring's Girls' Day festival. Cheerfully, my optimistic mother said, "We'll soon have a place to display them again."

The war brought sorrow to my family. My beloved oldest brother died in battle in Burma. I was sitting behind my mother when she read the notification of his death. I can still visualize her trembling body. These youthful experiences later motivated me to become a devoted peace activist.

HENDERSON • I sympathize with you. Our family didn't lose anyone in the war, but it was always close by. The Germans began bombing Bristol — about fifteen miles from Clevedon — in November 1940. We would see the whole sky light up from the fires. My father worked as a volunteer antiaircraft gunner. He would come home from his office in Bristol — about an hour commute — and then, after a very quick meal, would go to his station at the gun battery.

We had a spare room in our house, so people would be brought to us whose houses had been destroyed. Often our house was filled with other people. I had one little brother then, so all this was very hard work for my mother. Sometimes she was totally wiped out, yet she endured.

IKEDA • In those terrible days of war, caring for people outside the family must have been very hard indeed.

HENDERSON • On several occasions, our house was nearly hit. We had a sandbagged shelter, and I can remember the whistling bombs falling around us and then everything shaking. One night there was a tremendous explosion very nearby. The next morning, in the place where a close friend had lived, we found nothing except a hole in the ground. It was raining. That little girl, her family and everything were just gone. I was devastated.

IKEDA • In war, it is ordinary people who suffer and are sacrificed. Mr. Gorbachev insists that we of the war-children generation must expose the folly, inhumanity and irrationality of war. I agree entirely.

HENDERSON • I admire Mikhail Gorbachev and his current work for a better world, and I agree with his view of the responsibility of the war-children generation. The war affected me profoundly. Experiences like those certainly do make one a pacifist!

IKEDA • That is true. Unfortunately, however, wars persist. To end them, we must intensify public solidarity in the pursuit of peace. This is the heart of our SGI movement for human revolution. Because of my profound wish to rid the world of war, I opened my novel *The Human Revolution* with the following words: "Nothing is more barbarous than war. Nothing is more cruel."

The sequel, *The New Human Revolution*, opens with: "Nothing is as precious as peace; nothing brings more happiness. Peace is the basic point from which human progress begins."

Shaping life through hope and faith

HENDERSON • Those words convey a vitally important message. You took your war experiences and made something very positive out of them. I try to do the same in my own way.

You suggest that the twenty-first century will be a century of hope. To me, hope means an underlying attitude of faith — faith in life and the wonderful experiment that's been taking place on this planet for billions of years, and faith that it isn't going to stop with us.

IKEDA • To end that experiment would mean a defeat for human nature. Imperialism, colonialism and totalitarian Fascism dominated the first half of the twentieth century. The barren ideological conflict between capitalism and communism dragged on for most of the second half. Giving precedence to political and economic logic throughout the century resulted in inhuman consumerism and environmental destruction. More than ten years after the Cold War ended, confusion is only intensifying. Thinking people everywhere say that, if these go on unchecked — the stockpiling of weapons of mass destruction including nuclear weapons, environmental destruction on a steadily expanding worldwide scale and the rich–poor gap that widens as globalization proceeds — they will endanger the survival of our species and put an end to hope for new development.

HENDERSON • That's why we urgently need courageous reforms. You also have said that this century is the Century of Life and the Century of Women. I agree. The profound faith in the process of life shared by all human beings — men included — is particularly strong in women because of their involvement in giving birth and nurturing children.

12

IKEDA • Thank you for considerately including us men. But, as you say, there is a profound essential commonality between female characteristics and the processes of life. The Indian poet Rabindranath Tagore points this out with keen sensitivity. In his 1917 book *Personality*, he wrote: "All her forces instinctively work to bring things to some shape of fullness, for that is the law of life. In life's movement though nothing is final yet every step has its rhythm of completeness."[2]

HENDERSON • Wonderful words.

IKEDA • Tagore hoped that women could break with the old male-centered civilization of power and build a new civilization founded on cooperation and reciprocity like the all-fulfilling force of life. One of the mainstays of the Boston Research Center for the 21st Century, a peace-research organization that I founded, is an emphasis on the role of women. The director is a woman, Virginia Straus. I stipulated this out of my hope of mapping a course toward a Century of Life.

HENDERSON • They're doing wonderful work. For me, hope also means faith in the evolution of human consciousness. When you think that we began as Australopithecus and Neanderthals, we definitely have evolved — mentally as well as physically.

Even though wars continue and we make many mistakes, we must never give up hope that, in the very long view, we are becoming increasingly aware of our true situation as one species among many on a tiny planet. This evolution is very precious. The idea of hope growing out of faith in the life process indicates our evolutionary imperative to grow emotionally, mentally and spiritually. If we fail to grow in these ways, we'll destroy ourselves.

IKEDA • Human beings inherently possess the strength to overcome any hardship. Religions have traditionally taught the importance of such spiritual strength. This is Buddhism's point of origin. Shakyamuni Buddha taught us to strive to win happiness and peace, not outside but within ourselves.

The human being is not a frail wretch at the mercy of fate. Shakyamuni insisted that to change oneself now is to change the future on a vast scale. The Western impression that Buddhism is all about meditation is alien to the spirit of Shakyamuni. The goal of Nichiren Buddhism is neither escape from reality nor passive acceptance. It is to live strongly, proactively, in such a way as to refine one's own life and reform society through a constant exchange between the outside world and the individual's inner world.

HENDERSON • SGI members have impressed me strongly with their positive ways of coping with social problems. I assume that there is a philosophical basis to Nichiren Buddhism that makes it a socially engaged Buddhism.

IKEDA • Tsunesaburo Makiguchi, the Soka Gakkai's first president, was an educator and a practical person. The second president, Josei Toda, was a mathematics teacher as well as a businessman. Developing spirituality and listening to one's higher self are necessary but should be complemented by engagement in socially concerned activism.

HENDERSON • The optimistic SGI way of life is really wonderful. I have come in contact with many people in my line of work and can remember how, many years ago, people used to ask whether I was an optimist or a pessimist. I would answer that I have faith that humans are not terminally stupid! I look for positive trends and identify exemplary initiatives and inspiring people, whose effectiveness I try to help amplify through my writing, speeches and networking.

IKEDA • The important thing is not whether we are optimistic or pessimistic but rather that, while keeping a careful eye on reality, we are neither overwhelmed by it nor content with the status quo. We must keep the lamp of our ideals alight while being ready to pioneer uncharted paths. Faith in life and in the human spirit, such as yours, is the necessary foundation for this approach.

Adversity and inner glory

HENDERSON • As long as we keep our faith, adversity provides a favorable wind for growth. I think that stress is evolution's tool. As we are stressed by the environmental mistakes we're making, we are going to learn and move in more humane and ecologically sustainable directions.

If we lived in a perfect Garden of Eden where we didn't have to strive for anything, we might all go to sleep! We have created a lot of stress for ourselves by destroying ecosystems. We can use that stress as a signal, as a wake-up call, for the next stage of planetary awareness.

IKEDA • What you just said reminds me of something the British historian Arnold J. Toynbee said regarding the emergence and development of civilizations: "The natural environment itself does not determine the strengths or weaknesses of a race's creative powers. Rather the spring of civilizational creativity is the way it responds to environmental difficulties."[3]

HENDERSON • Yes, that would be his famous theory of challenge and response. In the context of today's state of global environmental destruction, the whole planet seems to be teaching us directly, reflecting back to us our mistakes. And that's the way people learn. This is why I feel close to people like David Loye, author of *Darwin's Lost Theory of Love* and Riane Eisler, author of *The Chalice and the Blade*. Robert Wright's *Non-Zero* speaks of similar causative patterns in evolution.

IKEDA • I have read *The Chalice and the Blade,* which argues that humanity must follow the way not of the control-type society symbolized by the blade of death and destruction but of the cooperative society symbolized by the chalice, which sustains and ennobles life.

HENDERSON • I enjoy books like *The Chalice and the Blade,* that explore humanity's potential for evolving consciousness, empathy and altruism.

As you know, many reductionist scientists at MIT, Harvard and elsewhere believe that the universe is random, an accident, chance. I could never believe such a thing. As I said earlier, hope can only come when you celebrate life and the life process, because life is so miraculous.

IKEDA • You have expressed that idea in poetry:

Pecos River Meditation *(excerpt)*

All life is sacred.
Truth that loses its meaning
In a welter of high-tech toys,
Trendy tricks and
Counterfeit spirituality.
Yet each one of us is sacred still,
Holy children of Gaia's love
And teeming plentitude.

How deep, deep we now must reach
To find our
Inner glory.[4]

HENDERSON • I am highly gratified that you find time to read my work and demonstrate such sincere interest in it.

True dialogue depends on knowing the other party well and listening carefully to what he or she says. You put these things into practice.

IKEDA • Thank you very much. My mentor, Josei Toda, thoroughly taught me that complete sincerity is the truly human way.

HENDERSON • The poem you just quoted continues:

Blest are those who find special ones
With whom to share the search. [5]

You are just such an important friend, and SGI members, who work hard for the future world, are my valued partners. I hope, as we continue this dialogue, that we can find a way to make this a Century of Life.

IKEDA • Dialogue is the key to the future. I intend our dialogue to be a light of hope illuminating our still uncharted era.

TWO

The University
Called Human Life

IKEDA • I've suggested that the twenty-first be named the Century of Women. Women have the wisdom and strength to lead society in the direction of good, of hope and of peace. In expanding his own nonviolence movement, Gandhi greatly relied on women. He said it is women who can teach pacific learning to a world that, while engaged in hostilities, nonetheless thirsts for the sweet dew of peace.

Women play a vital part in our SGI peace movement. I suspect that any organization or society that fails to recognize the importance of women in the years to come is doomed to decline.

HENDERSON • That is the trend of the times. I have insisted that the twenty-first ought to be a century of male–female partnership. I believed that an equal partnership between the sexes could restore balance to many human social activities, beginning with economics. Little by little, movement in this direction has been gaining impetus throughout the world, and it has already become an unstoppable current.

IKEDA • And you have taken the lead in starting off this new era.

Now I should like to hear your recollections of youth, the period during which the foundation of your personality was created. After graduating from high school, you boldly accumulated a great deal of experience.

HENDERSON • Yes, I did have many jobs. Instead of going straight to college after high school, I went out into society where my experience became a priceless asset. I suppose you could say I studied in the university called human life.

To tell the truth, I didn't like school much. I thought it was boring. I wanted to get out into the world as fast as I could. So I started working at sixteen. All of a sudden I was proud to be an adult, an independent woman. I left home, too, and lived with my older sister in a youth hostel. Still, I recommend women today get a college education.

IKEDA • "The university called human life" puts it beautifully. As you say, a college education is important. But a university is not all there is to learning and education. Learning from and assimilating life can be even more valuable. Book learning acquires meaning only in the context of society. Otherwise it never actually becomes part of our flesh and blood. I, too, can say this from experience.

Precisely what kinds of work did you do?

HENDERSON • I worked in a ladies clothing store in Bristol — at first, wrapping purchases in the back and later selling.

When I was there, a high wall separated the sales area from the back. Somebody out front would shout, "Wrap this!" and the purchase would come flying over that wall. I am pleased to say I became expert at folding garments. Before long, I was promoted to dealing directly with customers. It made me very happy to come out front.

We were by no means rich, but my sister and I enjoyed our lives and jobs. Every day was full.

IKEDA • In the burned ruins of Japan after World War II, I had to support our family. To do it, I worked during the day and attended classes at night. From an early age, I had many different jobs and learned a lot from all of them. I worked in an ironworks and in a printing plant. I did office work and managed a business. At one time, I was even editor of a boys' magazine. This varied experience became a great asset.

HENDERSON • Like you, I wanted to learn as much as possible, to travel and see the world. In those days, many British students worked their way around the world. After my sales work, I got a job in an English hotel at the reception desk and doing auditing. Then I went to work at a golf club in Bermuda and in other resorts around the Caribbean. In 1956, I went to New York, where I worked in an airline ticket office. I stayed there until I got married. So my early jobs were about learning my way around. All of them related to my search for the path I ought to follow.

IKEDA • You were on a voyage of self-searching as you worked.

HENDERSON • Yes. It was all very good experience I could apply to organizing citizens later. And it enabled me to move into an incredibly complex city like New York.

I had confidence that I could actually find out where everything was, who did what to whom, and how it all worked. Those experiences had a formative effect, not just on organizing but on theories, too. I learned that all people have potential, that everybody you see walking around — even a sales clerk like I was — has potential that, with effort, can expand.

IKEDA • Josei Toda ingrained in me the importance of never judging a book by its cover. It is impossible to tell from their exterior what future awaits people or what their mission may be. This is why Mr. Toda treated everybody exactly the same. He thoroughly disliked authoritarians, never flattered anyone, and was liberal with candid advice. At the same time, he was uniquely sympathetic to the hardships and sufferings of others. Some people scorned the Soka Gakkai, in its early years, as an assembly of the poor and sick. Mr. Toda said that was a title of honor.

HENDERSON • That attitude is really the starting point of the SGI, then. Very impressive. I agree with what you just said about not judging a book by its cover. Whoever they are and in whatever walk of life they find themselves, all people are, in a way, sacred to me. They're all sacred because they all have that spark of life.

IKEDA • Your line of thought mirrors that of Buddhism and many other religions. Did your parents or others have some influence on you in this connection?

HENDERSON • My parents were atheists. That was for the better. If you grow up and your parents tell you not to believe in anything, then, as a child, the first thing you do is look for things to believe in. I started to pay attention to various religious traditions in my early teens. The first was nature and the wonders of creation. I nonetheless ended up having tremendous faith in the spark of divinity that I expect to find in everybody. Because every religious tradition teaches the golden rule and tells you that the god is within, I couldn't understand why there is so much conflict among religions.

IKEDA • I absolutely understand what you mean. Returning to your youth experiences, what prompted you to leave England?

HENDERSON • I wanted to put my hotel skills to use elsewhere. I found my first overseas job in Bermuda and set out from Britain just after my twenty-first birthday. After gray and rainy England, I was entranced by the sun, the blue sea and sky, the brilliant flowers. All the time, I was reading, reading and reading.

Feeding the mind

IKEDA • I, too, loved reading more than anything when I was young. Whatever money I saved from my limited earnings I spent at bookstores buying both classics and new works. I stood in line for bestsellers. In my shabby notebook, I copied out and commented on passages that particularly struck me. I didn't limit myself to Japanese authors but read Plato's *Republic,* Rousseau's *Émile,* Montaigne's *Essays* and the works of Emerson. I also read the poetry of Goethe, Byron and many others. I loved biographies of great people. What did you like to read?

HENDERSON • There were lots of things, but I especially remember biographies of historical figures like Leonardo da Vinci. He was truly a complete human being. He was what we call today a Renaissance man. I loved his books of drawings of his inventions. Imagine! He actually invented an airplane in fifteenth-century Italy. I remember his famous self-portrait with the sad, beautiful eyes and the long beard.

IKEDA • Yes, it was painted in his later years. More than twenty-five years ago, I visited the house where he spent his last days. Mr. Toynbee and I had just finished our dialogue, and I was on a train from Paris to the Loire Valley. Ancient towns seemed to sleep in the spring sun on bucolic hillsides where sheep and cattle roamed through peaceful scenery. There in the midst of this peaceful scenery is Amboise Castle, a French king's royal residence, to which Leonardo had been invited. He is said to have died at the Manoir de Cloux nearby. On a copper plate on one of the manor house bedroom walls, his words are displayed:

> *The fulfilled life is long.*
> *Fulfilled days bring sweet sleep.*
> *A fulfilled life brings a tranquil death.*

I was deeply impressed.

HENDERSON • The words are a fitting symbol of his attitude toward life. I can't help feeling he was a man from the future living at a time that was inappropriate for him. I can remember looking into that face and thinking he must be a twentieth-century person. Can you imagine him living in the superstitious fifteenth century, when people didn't understand science or the scientific method? How lonely he must have been.

IKEDA • His loneliness was noble because it was born of tough spiritual power applied in the pursuit of limitless self-perfection. I share your great admiration for him. In a speech on his life and philosophy that I gave in June 1994 at the University of Bologna, I stressed the importance of determined self-control and ceaseless upward flight. In the hope that students will strive to be as brave as he and spread their spiritual wings in the sky of the twenty-first century, we have installed a statue of Leonardo da Vinci in the main building at Soka University.

Reviving the poetic spirit

HENDERSON • That's wonderful. Another of my favorites is the beautiful book of Persian poetry called *The Rubaiyat of Omar*

Khayyam, translated into English by Edward Fitzgerald. It expresses a fundamental philosophy in concise quatrains.

IKEDA • Not only was Omar Khayyam a fine poet, he was a mathematician, astronomer, doctor and specialist in Islamic Law as well. His versatility earned him the title of the Persian Leonardo da Vinci. His poems are more than songs of pleasure and pain. As you say, they contain a brilliant inner philosophy. What other poets do you like?

HENDERSON • I love all of the English romantic poets — Keats and Wordsworth who, like Thackeray, lived for a while in Clevedon. But Shelley is my favorite.

IKEDA • I love his passionate poetry, too. His famous line from "Ode to the West Wind," "If winter comes, can spring be far behind?" encouraged me in many of the struggles of my youth. Shelley said that the poet, through his work, can foster greatness in people and become a trustworthy friend, a pioneer who can influence thoughts and social systems. Today, the loss of the poetic spirit concerns me. Poetry inspires because it is in sympathy with nature and the cosmos.

HENDERSON • I believe in the power of poetry. That's why I include poems in my books on economics and the environment. Businesspeople are conspicuous among today's leaders. If they and politicians cannot embrace the poetic spirit, then poets will have to become our leaders. When I speak of poets, I mean people with vision. Some poets are also very practical; for example, poet and playwright Václav Havel, the former president of the Czech Republic, on whose Forum 2000 dialogues on globalization I served as an advisor. Mr. Havel is a courageous leader.

IKEDA • I agree entirely. If authority stands for animal nature, poetry symbolizes human nature. Today people's hearts are cold. I believe that poetry has the power to warm them and to revive the youthful force of life.

I write poetry practically every day. I once wrote these lines to a French friend.

> *Poetry is sculpted inner truth,*
> *The flaring flame of earnestness.*
> *An offering of poetry is*
> *An offering of life.*

HENDERSON • The work of a poet like you is important. Poetry and all other writing have true meaning only when they establish reverberations between the minds of writer and reader. Many books have influenced me. Among them was *The Tao of Physics* by Fritjof Capra, written in the mid-1970s. It explores a way toward science harmonious with life and nature, based upon Oriental thought, and it fit everything I believed so well that it left me almost in tears.

Books are really wonderful, especially when the reader is close to the author. Fritjof Capra became a good friend and remains one today.

IKEDA • Reading entails both careful self-reflection and a dialogue with a book's author.

HENDERSON • Yes. There's nothing more interactive than a book. If you look at the books in my library, you'll see that in every one of them I have asked questions and underlined bits. In the fronts of books I list all the main points. A book is a very active way to develop your ideas and your philosophy. Most television programming, on the other hand, is too passive. The Internet makes me feel like I'm getting information from a fire hose! There's too much. But a book you take at your own pace, pick it up and put it down. It becomes a friend.

IKEDA • I always tell young people that early contact with the great classics plays an important role in spiritual development. While stressing the importance of reading, I try to quote passages from various works. In a January 2001 paper on education,[1] I dealt mainly with topics like bullying in school and violence. I also stressed the importance of reading for the following reasons: 1) in a sense, the experiences gained from reading are miniatures of real-life experiences; 2) accumulated reading serves as a barrier protecting young spirits from the potentially destructive influence of virtual reality; and 3) reading provides an excellent opportunity for young and old alike to think deeply about the bigger issues of life without being swallowed up in everyday affairs. I mentioned how important it is for parents and teachers to read aloud to children. Now the Soka Gakkai is promoting a campaign among mothers with small children to read aloud to them for ten minutes a day.

HENDERSON • Yes, children should become accustomed to reading at an early age. My mother's influence made me love books. It was the warmest, most pleasant and wonderful thing because reading time was when she would take us on her knee. I carried on the tradition with my own daughter, who loves to read. I think reading is the best self-development there is.

Life-changing encounters

IKEDA • I'm moved by your words. Certainly, a mother's warmth is vital. Throughout life, we encounter people who affect us significantly. I would be interested to know what encounters of this kind you had during your youth.

My own meeting with Josei Toda determined my fate. The education I received from him has made me what I am today. Mr. Toda was not only an outstanding educator but also a superb philosopher and activist in matters of faith. Today his thoughts and deeds form the basis of the Soka Gakkai International peace movement. The far-sighted vision of his "Declaration Against Nuclear Weapons" and his championing of planetary citizenship are now steadily gaining the attention they deserve.

HENDERSON • When did you first meet him?

IKEDA • On August 14, 1947, when I was nineteen. At the time, I was searching for reliable guidelines for the rest of my life. At the invitation of a friend, I attended a Soka Gakkai discussion meeting led by Mr. Toda.

Attracted by his clear words, great assurance, deeply considerate love of youth and relaxed and sincere personality, I was eager to get to know him better. Later, learning how he had been imprisoned by the militarist fascists along with his own mentor and teacher, Tsunesaburo Makiguchi, the first Soka Gakkai president, and how, even after being imprisoned, he had remained unwaveringly true to his convictions, I concluded that he was the person I wanted for my teacher.

HENDERSON • It moves me deeply to hear about your early search for direction and that you found your spiritual path through your own striving rather than childhood inculcation in any religion. It was a fateful encounter.

IKEDA • Yes, it was. At the time, he ran a publishing company. I quit my job to go to work for him and began a new public and private life, moving forward by his side. Later, when his business fell on hard times, I gave up everything else to help.

This meant discontinuing night classes. But Mr. Toda became my private tutor, holding study sessions early every weekday morning and on Sundays. For several years, he instructed me in government, economy, science, law, literature and astronomy. What I learned from him was of incalculable use to me in later years.

His unbending determination to rid the world of misery and the fierce intensity of his desire to bring happiness to the unfortunate impressed me profoundly.

HENDERSON • I understand that when you first encountered Mr. Toda, it was his humanity rather than his theories that impressed you. I remember the first time I met Elise Boulding, I was impressed with her lovely personality. She is a famous sociologist, and her ideas found expression in Kenneth Boulding's work as well. She was with her husband, Kenneth, when I met them together for the first time in Colorado. I had read Kenneth Boulding's *Beyond Economics* in the late 1960s and had first met him in Australia in 1973.

IKEDA • Both were intellectuals who worked hard for the cause of world peace. He presented me with a copy of his *Beyond Economics*. Both the Bouldings were good enough to show interest in the SGI popular movement. Unfortunately, Kenneth Boulding died in 1993. Elise Boulding, of course, is widely known as a specialist in peace culture, a key concept for the twenty-first century. She often cooperates in a most encouraging way with projects of the Boston Research Center for the 21st Century.

Learning from the experts

HENDERSON • I learned a lot from those fine people. I had begun writing my own critique of conventional economics in 1968 in a series of articles in the *Harvard Business Review*. Boulding's work was a great help — as was Robert Heilbroner's classic, *The Worldly Philosophers* — in forming my ideas of how to correct economics.

About that time, like you, I wanted to go to college. But you had to support Mr. Toda's business. As you say, your great reward was to receive individual tutoring from this great man. For me, organizing people and groups to combat air pollution seemed more important than college; and my first priority was raising my child.

IKEDA • So you read and studied on your own.

HENDERSON • Yes. I wrote to many colleges asking if they had courses on how ecology relates to economics, biology, sociology, anthropology and physics. When I learned that there were no such courses — this was the 1960s — I decided to continue studying on my own.

The best part of learning is the personal relationship between the teacher and the learner. Most of my teachers were authors. When I read their work, I often had a tremendous desire to meet them, which I found was not so difficult to do.

IKEDA • When you say the best part of learning is the personal relationship between teacher and learner, you penetrate to the essence of education. On this point, Ralph Waldo Emerson is quoted in an essay titled "Emerson on Education": "Happy the natural college thus self-instituted around every natural teacher; the young men of Athens around Socrates; of Alexander around

Plotinus; of Paris around Abelard; of Germany around Fichte, or Niebuhr, or Goethe: in short the natural sphere of every leading mind."[2]

For me the natural college was "Toda University." You formed a natural college through direct contacts with the authors of the books you read. How did you get to meet them?

HENDERSON • It was really quite easy. I found out their addresses and wrote to them. I expressed how meaningful their books were to me and then referred to passages for clarification. I developed mentoring relationships through the mail. That was how I first got in touch with Elise Boulding, Robert Heilbroner, Barbara Ward and many other writers, including Linus Pauling.

IKEDA • A very good idea. It worked because your sincerity and fervor transmitted themselves to the people with whom you made contact. Your experience should be a good reference for the readers of our dialogue.

While visiting one of the exhibitions devoted to Linus Pauling that the SGI held in America, you said that, without such exhibitions, mistaken impressions of him might have persisted in history. People who are ahead of their times often meet criticism and oppression. Since you are always ahead of your times, I suspect this has been your lot, too.

What books and people made an especially strong impact on you before you started your work in civic movements?

HENDERSON • One of the most formative influences for me was Betty Friedan, a leader of the women's liberation movement, who wrote *The Feminine Mystique.* I encountered it in 1963, before I started Citizens for Clean Air. Through that book, she spoke to me, as she did to so many millions of women in the United States. There we were, sitting in our little houses and being told that the main things in our lives were to cook nicely, keep house, and all that. But I knew that my life was about much more, yet I felt guilty, because I had a husband and child. Later, in the 1960s, I met Barbara Marx Hubbard, the philosopher of the conscious evolution of humanity, whose first book, *The Hunger of Eve,* called on me and many thousands of women to explore our highest purpose. Barbara and I have remained "soul sisters" ever since.

IKEDA • Like Simone de Beauvoir's *The Second Sex,* published shortly after World War II, *The Feminine Mystique* was widely read in Japan. A wife and the mother of three, Friedan started her movement from her own doubts about the way she lived.

HENDERSON • That's true. I didn't want to shortchange my husband or my child, but I felt there must be more in life than being a housewife. We all thought of ourselves as housewives; but Betty Friedan told us, if that's all we were, it was because of a social conspiracy. She said, "You are a fully fledged human being and you can be anything you want." A part of me had always believed that. Yet social pressure meant that, once a woman got married, her independent life was over. From then on, she was in service to her husband and her children, and that was the proper thing to do. If you had any other ambition, you were neither a good wife nor a good mother — and you were a bit strange. I'd been married for about five years when Friedan's book came out and profoundly changed my views. This readied me for my encounter with Barbara Marx Hubbard, whose recent books are *Conscious Evolution: Awakening the Power of Our Social Potential* and *Emergence: The Shift from Ego to Essence.*

IKEDA • Friedan's ideas had a big impact on all of American society. Her great significance was in raising the question of how women should live and perfect themselves. I know many superb women who work hard for their families and, at the same time, contribute greatly to society. I believe that making the best use of women's viewpoints and applying their plentiful sensibility and benevolence in all fields are necessary, vital elements for a society that will be kind to humanity and the environment.

THREE

Saving the Mother of Life

Soot on the skin, fire in the heart

IKEDA • The civic movement dealing with New York's environmental problems grew from a core group called Citizens for Clean Air, formed in 1964, in which you played a central role. I understand that soot stains on your daughter's skin stimulated you to form this group.

HENDERSON • Yes. I knew something about bad air because I had lived until age five in polluted Bristol and had coughed a lot, especially when pollution was bad. New York's air pollution was bad. The concrete in a park near our apartment was black with soot. My daughter, Alexandra, used to go there to play; and when she came home, there was soot on her skin. I had to put her in the bath and scrub her to get it off. In addition to soot, smoke from thousands of garbage incinerators made the air smell bad.

I knew this represented a health threat for everyone, especially children. Mostly what galvanized me to act was considering this threat in light of what I knew about the great smog in London in 1952, when four thousand more people than usual died in a week.

IKEDA • A most painful incident. I have heard that Londoners coined the term *smog* by combining *smoke* and *fog*. When the smog was bad, unusual harm from air pollution began to spread.

HENDERSON • Yes. That stuck in my mind. I thought, well, here's the potential for the same thing to happen in New York, and yet New Yorkers seemed completely unaware that smog can kill. At that time, as I mentioned, I had read *Silent Spring* as well as Barry Commoner's *The Closing Circle*. Inspired by Rachel Carson's struggle and lectures by Dr. Commoner, I decided that I had to act. But I was only an ordinary housewife. What could I do? I began asking mothers of other children who played in that same park if they didn't think the air was bad. Before long a small group was formed.

IKEDA • You did what we do in the SGI: continually engage in open-minded dialogue. We form small local groups, which gradually grow into civic movements. Small group discussions are a Soka Gakkai tradition dating back to first president Makiguchi and continuing today in SGI organizations around the world. In the words of Nichiren, "Plant a seed, and it will multiply into many." One person taking action stimulates another to follow suit. In this way the movement spreads outward courageously in multiple ripples.

Letters win support

HENDERSON • Everything starts with person-to-person friendship and trust. I was nervous at first. It took courage. But I knew that letting the present situation continue was dangerous; so I talked to people one by one and made friends. As we discussed things, we came to the conclusion that it was

36

our civic duty to do something for the many people living in the city.

I began writing letters during my daughter's afternoon naps — first to Robert Wagner, who was then mayor of New York City. I had just got my U.S. citizenship. I saw that, unlike in England where I grew up, American citizens traditionally speak out and act. It is a good tradition, and I was proud to follow it.

IKEDA • Did Mayor Wagner answer your letter?

HENDERSON • He replied that the pollution I thought I saw was really just mist rolling in from the sea! This caused me to investigate further, and I found the city actually had an office of smoke control. When I phoned them to report smoke coming from nearby chimneys, I was told that they measured soot particles in the city's air each day. So I requested that the TV networks broadcast air-pollution data daily on weather forecasts. By this time, our group had about ten members. I took up the task of writing letters to major television networks. When I learned that broadcasting fell under the jurisdiction of the Federal Communications Commission in Washington, I wrote to the chairman. Then I wrote to Nelson Rockefeller, governor of New York State.

IKEDA • What did you say in the letters?

HENDERSON • I included information about New York City smoke-control devices and requested that television broadcasts include daily measurements under FCC requirements that they "should broadcast in the public interest, convenience, and necessity," stipulated by a 1934 act of congress. Replies came to me from the FCC's chairman Newton Minow and from Governor Rockefeller, both asking me to keep them informed of the TV networks' responses.

I then photocopied these letters and sent them to TV network chiefs. In a few weeks, I was stunned to receive a call from an ABC-TV News vice president.

IKEDA • I can see how you'd be surprised.

HENDERSON • Yes, I could hardly believe it. He asked if I was the woman who wanted to put a New York air-pollution index on TV weather programs. I said yes, and to my amazement he said the network liked the idea and was researching it. One month later, the New York Air Pollution Index, based on primitive soot measurements, was on the air. Three months later, all TV stations, most radio stations and local newspapers were covering the index.

This began to stimulate public awareness, which led to the growth of Citizens for Clean Air. Similar indexes began being broadcast in cities other than New York, too.

Making waves

IKEDA • As we say, ten thousand waves start with the first wave. The first step is important. How did you feel when you saw your movement making headway?

HENDERSON • I felt we could really change the situation if we continued making efforts. As we persevered, Citizens for Clean Air helped pass several pollution control laws. Encouraged by these early developments, I took part in civic movements in other fields.

At the start, ordinary people often think projects are impossible. They are afraid that the obstacles are too big. But, as we showed, a way can be found when we combine forces. Not all walls are so thick and strong that we can't find a doorway somewhere and make a breakthrough.

IKEDA • Your words are all the more significant because they are backed by real deeds.

HENDERSON • Thank you. As you know, one has to have a thick skin to be a civic activist and a global citizen. The important lessons are persistence and continually reaching out to people — even powerful politicians and business leaders — and appealing to that "God" within each of us: the higher self.

This is what I admire about you and the members of the Soka Gakkai International I have met around the world. They are a highly organized and persistent group of people. I know lots of groups that are spirituality motivated but can make nothing happen. That's why I'm so impressed to see SGI members making things happen, such as their great work for peace and the banning of nuclear weapons.

IKEDA • Thank you for your warm words. Did anyone influence you to keep going?

Norman Cousins, a practical idealist

HENDERSON • Norman Cousins became my first real role model as a world citizen. As you know, he was a founder of the World Federalists and a publisher and editor-in-chief of the magazine *Saturday Review*. Your published dialogue with Cousins[1] revealed that, like you, he was fully engaged in the world. He had a vision of a planetary future with no war, a vision we shared. I was enthralled by it and by his down-to-earth nature.

IKEDA • Norman Cousins was a valued friend. He had a very broad mind and a tremendous sense of responsibility. I can still hear him saying: "The greatest tragedy of life is not death but living death. The death of the inner self during life. This is the most fearsome of tragedies. The important thing is what we do while alive."

This seems to epitomize his way of life as, even while struggling against grave illness, he traveled far and wide in the name of peace and human rights.

He was a man of universal interests. Even in this age of specialization, there are still people who try to be complete personalities, Renaissance personalities.

HENDERSON • Another thing that impressed me so much about Norman Cousins was the multiplicity of his skills and dimensions. He brought his spirituality into the practical world. He was an idealist, but a practical idealist. That's what I see in you also. You are a complete person, as I always aspire to be.

One aspect of a whole person is care; another is righteous — though always nonviolent — anger, which has often motivated me. I'm talking about the righteous indignation that less-than-human behavior or inhuman social evil evokes. As Mr. Cousins's quote about death points out, it is an indignity for any human being not to be allowed to live up to his or her full potential. I've been righteously angry at politicians for taking huge sums of money from special interests. Righteous indignation is acceptable as a motivator; it's energizing.

IKEDA • Nichiren wrote that wrath can be either good or bad. Self-centered anger generates evil, but wrath at social injustice becomes the driving force for reform. Strong language that censures and combats a great evil often awakens adverse reactions from society, but this must not intimidate those who believe

40

they are right. The lion is a lion because he roars.

Josei Toda always said: "Don't be afraid of authority. Don't be afraid of anybody. Fear of authorities can destroy democracy and sacrifice the ordinary people, in whom sovereignty must always rest."

While consistently demonstrating the utmost foresight in your proposals on environmental issues, you have been dubbed one of the most dangerous women in the United States.

HENDERSON • That's true. It hurt sometimes. But I felt I ought to say out loud what I had to say. Nobody could stop me. From the start of the movement I assumed there would be difficulties. As a matter of fact, I find difficulties exciting.

Winning the public mind

IKEDA • Very courageous words. The SGI has grown as it has because, especially in our early days, our women members had that kind of spirit.

I'd like to hear a bit more about your association with Norman Cousins. When did you first meet him?

HENDERSON • I met him at the very early stage of organizing for Citizens for Clean Air. That must have been about 1964. He had been appointed by the new mayor of New York, John Lindsay, to head up a task force on air pollution. I sat right down and wrote him a letter. I told him that he didn't need to do a study about air pollution because our group already knew what it was about — a lack of public education. I said, "I'd like to come to your office." Norman became a great friend. I wrote an article for his *Saturday Review* about my first visit to Japan in 1973.

IKEDA • What influence did your association with him have on your movement?

HENDERSON • The next step in the clean-air program was public education. In this, I learned invaluable lessons and gained a key ally in Norman Cousins, who opened many doors for me.

We had to shake up the administration and the mass media. At the same time, we had to teach each New Yorker about the fundamentals of the problem. We decided on a campaign to explain the seriousness of the situation. We needed to advertise but had no money. I decided to try finding a public-spirited advertising company that would undertake the project for free. I went from one company on Madison Avenue to another but was usually disappointed.

IKEDA • How many companies did you try?

HENDERSON • About twenty. After I'd been to every likely company, I made up my mind to try one more and then give up this angle if I was turned down. I found one, the newly formed Carl Ally Agency, which agreed to help. It was a foggy day, and the air was badly polluted. To my surprise, I was shown into the executive suite where I met the young president, Carl Ally. I told him about New York's dangerous air pollution and that calling attention to it was very important, but that our citizens group had no money. He called the people in charge of such projects and told them I wanted an advertising campaign done free. They all agreed that such volunteer work was good and said they'd go ahead.

IKEDA • Again, your perseverance paid off.

HENDERSON • Yes, it did. I was delighted. In a few months, a beautiful, truthful advertising campaign was created. Then we had to find sponsors to get it out. The story about the year it took me to find other allies and finally get the public-education advertising campaign running in the New York media is too long to tell here.

I must say, however, that Norman Cousins was the key to turning our tough situation around. Thanks to his efforts, New York television, radio and newspapers accepted our public-education ads. Finally our efforts bore fruit when the city council passed two laws on air pollution and regulated several pollution sources.

IKEDA • In recognition of this achievement, in 1967, the New York Medical Association conferred the Citizen of the Year Award on you. Then when the federal government passed anti-air-pollution legislation, you were among the civic-movement representatives who met with President Lyndon Johnson.

In your work you must have had arguments with many politicians and businessmen. How did you react to such encounters?

HENDERSON • In the battle against air pollution, I did encounter lots of opposition from officials who mostly hoped I'd just go away.

The hardest to deal with are corporations, because they are very calculating. For instance, the vice president for public relations of a corporation takes me to lunch and buys me a glass of wine. I tell him his corporation must change its polluting ways, and he agrees. Later, of course, I realize that he and his company have no intention of doing anything.

At first, I was very naïve. I recognized that my struggle is a great one; many social forces are much stronger and richer than me. I have to deal with them with all my heart and mind. I learned that you cannot deal with corporations unless you organize or own lots of their stock. That was when I discovered the importance of organizing not only consumers but also shareholders, which I did later.

IKEDA • In Book Twelve of *Paradise Lost*, Milton wrote:

> *[W]ith good*
> *still overcoming evil, and by small*
> *accomplishing great things, by things deemd weak*
> *Subverting worldly strong. . . .*

In a splendid way, you subverted worldly strong by overcoming various trials. No doubt you had your share of hard times. What was the worst for you?

HENDERSON • The worst thing was getting letters accusing me of being a communist. That was very hurtful because it was the furthest thing from my mind. I was not a bit political, really. Quite often there was even worse.

My first husband is a very kind and nice man. I learned a lot about journalism from him while he was an editor for *The Wall Street Journal*. By the time I started my movement, he was working for IBM. People who objected to my work would write to the president of IBM to tell him the wife of a company staff member was a communist. That was awfully difficult, because I didn't want to hurt his career.

IKEDA • There are always people who use cowardly methods like cold, irrelevant criticism. For many decades, I have been subjected to a storm of heartless criticism and false and groundless rumors of various kinds.

The whole civic movement started because of your daughter's experience with soot in the air. How has she reacted to your work?

44

HENDERSON • When she was younger, she didn't really know about it. When she was a teenager, she was like most teenagers. She would say to her friends, "My mother's really a bit crazy." It must have been a burden sometimes to have a mother who led civic movements. But once she grew up she came to understand and support my way of life. She asked, "How did you hold on so long in the face of people thinking you were crazy?" I am very proud of her. She has a career as a therapist and social worker as well as being a wonderful mother.

IKEDA • She witnessed what you were doing. And I am sure that she and your grandchild will inherit your noble spirit. You have stood by your convictions all your life. What do you think it takes to make a success of a civic movement?

HENDERSON • There are several important elements. First, the problem must be serious and apparent to everybody. Second, you have to recruit people to help you and lots of volunteers. Third, you must become a world-class expert on the problem with which you're dealing. Investigate and research every pronouncement you make. All the data you quote must be checked against originals. And it's vital that what you say be convincing.

Make use of the power of the mass media in a good sense. And, as we have already said over and over, don't give up no matter what difficulties you face. If you consistently assert something and it is right, the times are sure to come around to it.

IKEDA • I agree entirely. Your words reveal how much passion and meticulous care you have devoted to your undertakings. Everything you say is absolutely convincing.

HENDERSON • Thank you. Actually, however, there is one more important point.

IKEDA • What is that?

HENDERSON • A civic movement must have a philosophy. Each of its participants must have a noble spirituality to fall back on. The SGI certainly has such a philosophy. How has it grown into this influential worldwide organization? I will be your student on this one.

IKEDA • We made the human revolution of each individual our basic point. One must transcend the smaller self and devote his or her life to large goals, for other people and for society. Going beyond the framework of a single religious organization, we constantly reexamine what we should do as a social entity while extending our people's movement worldwide based on three pillars — peace, culture and education. The philosophical quality you mention must be refined through actual practice in society. Our orientation is rooted in the Mahayana bodhisattva way of life.

HENDERSON • What do you mean by the bodhisattva way of life?

IKEDA • Buddhist philosophy divides life into ten stages, which we refer to as the Ten Worlds. The Bodhisattva world is the ninth, just below the Buddha world. The bodhisattva nature can be interpreted from many angles, but most important is the willing and spontaneous vow, summoned forth from one's entire being, to set others on the road to happiness. This vow is not just wishful thinking; it is a lofty declaration of volunteerism. The bodhisattva remains active in the ordinary world, watching over the unhappy and suffering. The bodhisattva is ready to plunge into the rough waves to save the drowning and put them all on the great vessel that will carry them to safety. In this sense, the bodhisattva is the ultimate humanist. As is said in the Lotus Sutra, the bodhisattva is like a lotus flower blooming in purity out of the muddy water.

HENDERSON • This is a beautiful vision.

IKEDA • I once lectured on the bodhisattva practice at Claremont McKennna College near Los Angeles. At that time, Linus Pauling also spoke. He commented that extending a sincere helping hand to those in trouble—that sort of bodhisattva-like behavior — is wonderful proof of being human and the key to evoking affinity across borders. The SGI has grown into an indomitable worldwide organization because it prizes every individual.

Having devoted my life to this philosophy, I constantly urge our leaders to embrace it. We have no secret stratagem. Our members encourage one another and accept the challenges posed by their individual reformation of character. Each person's triumph over his or her "lesser self" propels social development and ultimately influences human history. This is the core of our human revolution movement.

FOUR

A New Economics

IKEDA • I've heard that you are an active advisor to governmental and institutional organizations in more than thirty nations. Also, your articles are dispatched to more than four hundred newspapers throughout the world. In Japan, the monthly magazine *Nikkei Ecology* has carried one of your articles.

HENDERSON • Yes, I introduced my view on the Japanese economy. I believe that Japan has great potential.

IKEDA • Your views on economics are drawing worldwide attention, especially your new concept of the "love economy."

Now I should like to turn to the way you have used your experiences in New York to evolve what you call the new economics.

HENDERSON • When I started studying the topic, I found that the very base of economic theory was wrong and that it had distorted society.

It is very important to improve the environment so that all people — especially children — can breathe clean air. But whenever I consulted big business about it, the people in charge would say my ideas were impossible because they cost too much money. As I listened to rebuffs like this, I began feeling that there was some mistake in the very economic principles that everybody took for granted.

IKEDA • You keenly observed that there should be something in economics about protecting the environment and making people happier.

HENDERSON • My activism for the environment and my studies in biology, ecology and thermodynamics first led me to doubt traditional economics. What I learned from those studies seemed too different from conventional economics and its explanations of things. So I decided to do my own study and research. Since universities didn't offer the kinds of courses I wanted, I started reading relevant books in libraries.

IKEDA • I admire the way you moved from doubting to studying and then to concrete action. Still, as a housewife and mother, you must have found it difficult. What hurdles did you encounter?

HENDERSON • Nothing special. We were living in a small apartment that was easy to keep clean. My husband was off to work at eight in the morning and came back at about six in the evening. My daughter was still small and napped for two or three hours in the afternoon. That schedule left me free time in which to study. When that was not enough, I studied at night after everybody was in bed, or I got up early in the morning. I didn't find any of this difficult because I enjoy studying.

"Economics is not a science"

IKEDA • Encouraging words! At first when you tried to discuss the matter with them, isn't it true that the specialists haughtily scorned you as an uninformed amateur and a housewife with no inkling of how economic mechanisms work?

HENDERSON • Yes. On one television program, an economist sitting next to me said, "She is a nice lady, but she doesn't know a thing about economics." I was not about to give in, and such criticisms only made up my mind to study further. Then, when I met such economists again, I'd know enough economics to counter their arguments. Time and time again, I bought lots of books and studied some more, embracing more disciplinary perspectives that also challenge economics.

IKEDA • I can see you are one who is determined not to lose.
　What are your impressions of having worked on government inquiry panels?

HENDERSON • Many times in public hearings, I witnessed economists hired by companies use economic theories and tools — like cost–benefit analyses — to obscure key issues, demote ecological and social values, and confuse both citizens and politicians. Then, when I was appointed to the Advisory Council of the OTA — the U.S. Congress Office of Technology Assessment — in 1974, I saw a similar use of economics to advocate narrow corporate and other special interests and to promote laissez-faire policies that allowed business to harm the public interest.
　Serving on this congressional body until 1980 gave me valuable insights on how economics, which is *not* a science, became the dominant policy discipline in governments around the globe. I have been trying ever since to break the stranglehold the economics profession has on public policy.

Challenging Nobel laureates

IKEDA • You really scolded those wily specialists and scholars. You said their ideas were false, and that they themselves often didn't believe in such crude models. You called them birds in gilded cages of their own manufacture.

Your first book, *Creating Alternative Futures*, published in 1978, was highly influential in the search for a new economics.

HENDERSON • The book reflects a systematic approach from the viewpoints of ecology and thermodynamics as well as sociology and psychology. I had mentors in ecology like Barry Commoner; Eugene Odum, with whom I served on the OTA Advisory Council; and his brother Howard Odum, whose courses I took at the University of Florida. A standard text in the field, Eugene Odum's *Basics of Ecology* is highly regarded all over the world. Howard Odum is known for the ecology of social systems he has evolved through fresh ideas and meticulous logic. I learned thermodynamics from Nicholas Georgescu-Roegen, pioneer of the entropy concept, and his monumental *Entropy Law and the Economic Process*. All this stood me in good stead for the intellectual challenges of debating Nobel Prize winners in physics and medicine and corporate CEOs serving with me on the OTA Advisory Council.

IKEDA • So you tempered your own theories by reading the works of these world-famous people and meeting with them personally.

HENDERSON • That's right. From 1974 until 1978, I also served on the Research Applied to National Needs Committee of the National Science Foundation and the National Academy of Engineering Committee on Public Engineering Policy. Meeting and debating so many famous scientists from so many fields was daunting and kept me studying night and day. This was my alternative doctorate study period, during which I honed my debating skills and verified my critiques of traditional economics.

IKEDA • What a tremendous effort. Elise Boulding describes you as self-schooled, correctly saying, "She apprenticed herself, learning experientially in the middle of the action-arena when others were sitting in classrooms."[1] People who recognized your farsightedness at an early stage now say that, at last, the times are catching up with you.

Alternatives that can be corroborated

HENDERSON • Thank you. It's just that I have consistently said the same thing. Today, the field of economics is responding to the chorus of interdisciplinary criticisms that I began in the United States and that Ernst "Fritz" Schumacher had been making simultaneously in the United Kingdom. The old economics pollutes the environment and makes a lot of people poor and miserable, but not everybody. Many do very well, including those with power and inherited wealth and the special interests that influence politics and resource allocation. Globalization on such economic models is widening the gap between rich and poor.

I considered it my job to refute recognized experts because a lot of them lacked a holistic view. All I did was develop a more holistic view, which spurred my interest in making myself into a whole human being. You can't have a holistic view without being a whole person.

IKEDA • I agree. Progressive subdivision and specialization in scholarly fields may make it impossible for people to assume an overall viewpoint. You did not stop at merely criticizing conventional economics. You actually worked out new economics to oppose it.

Time and again in my youth, Josei Toda told me how important concrete proposals are to the peace and progress of humanity. "Even if not immediately realizable," he would say, "concrete projects become sparks from which the light of peace spreads. Empty theorizing is always futile. Concrete proposals are the pillars for their own realization and the roof that protects the people."

Since my mentor's doctrine was engraved on my mind as a young man, I have studied and reflected a great deal. The peace proposals I make every year on January 26, SGI Day, have evolved from this study and reflection. Furthermore, I am devoted entirely to their realization. One of my proposals in 2002 was to make active use of the energy of sunshine and wind.

HENDERSON • Wonderful. That's one issue I am particularly concentrating upon. I gather how much you appreciated Mr. Toda as a whole human being. It's no good living in your head, talking about theories that have never been tested. Putting out concrete proposals, as you say, is best. It's all well and good to have theories, but you want to see if you can organize a bake sale around your theories. Will anybody come and buy your cakes?

IKEDA • Empirical corroboration is essential. Tsunesaburo Makiguchi, the Soka Gakkai founding president and a superb educator, believed that in the learning situation, empirical corroboration is indispensable. Mr. Makiguchi taught and practiced the Buddhist concept of the three proofs that while teachings must certainly be verified in written form and be theoretically convincing, most important is that their correctness is corroborated in real life. He also said that we should all seek a way of life that enables both the self and others to enjoy happiness and peace. Such is the life of great good to create value for society of which he spoke.

In the SGI tradition, testimonials corroborating the truth of our teachings are given at the small discussion meetings I have already mentioned. In Mr. Makiguchi's time, those meetings were called Discussion Meetings for Empirical Corroboration of the Life of Great Good.

HENDERSON • That's very interesting. I doubted traditional economic theories because, although they look good on paper, they often just don't work in the real world. People would tell me we couldn't afford to clean up pollution. I knew they were wrong, because I knew pollution would make people sick, and ill health is very costly for everyone. I thought it was crazy that there was so much theoretical effort on the part of economists to deny the evidence of my senses. I could smell and see the pollution! Economists ignored these social and environmental costs as "externalities" — an example of a Freudian slip.

IKEDA • It's like the Procrustean bed on which human beings would be cruelly stretched or shortened to fit. Trying to make the real world fit their theories is a folly; it indicates something wrong in modern human spirituality. This can invite ideological rigidity and atrocities of the kind the twentieth century witnessed. It is to give first priority to statistics, to ignore the joys and sorrows of individuals for the sake of a mold-cast image of humanity.

HENDERSON • That's the root of the environmental problem. No theory can get you to deny the evidence of your senses. Economists' theories often do not work because they're enormous simplifications of real human behavior. They assume that we're all from the same cookie cutter. It was so obvious that their theories did not take into account people's values. They would always say that economics is a science and economists are value-free, yet their economics is normative to the very core. It's all about their own values and their denial of the values of others. If they are incapable of retracting their own views, why not come out in the open and admit that economics is just politics in disguise?

Of course, my ideas horrified economists; and, as you mentioned, a corporate public relations newsletter called me one of the most dangerous women in the United States. I am proud of it.

IKEDA • It would have been more accurate to call you one of the most advanced women in the United States. As confusion deepens in our era, your ideas assume increasingly weighty significance.

At the State of the World Forum held in New York in September 2000, former Dutch prime minister and current UN High Commissioner for Refugees Ruud Lubbers introduced you by saying that, over the years, he has read your books repeatedly. He called you the parent of the new economics. In the past, he said, people criticized your ideas as exaggerated, outspoken and impractical. But the time has come to turn a serious ear to your message.

HENDERSON • I wasn't the only one subjected to criticism. For a long time, my spiritual mentor and friend, Fritz Schumacher, was subjected to heartless criticism. But he merely pursued his own ideas, saying it was all right for people to call him a "crank" because the crank is a useful device that creates revolutions!

Dr. Schumacher influenced me profoundly. We were good friends. His was an economics for peace organized on the idea that human beings share life among themselves and with all other living beings.

Meeting with Dr. Schumacher

IKEDA • "A crank is a useful device that creates revolutions." That is terrific. When did you first meet Dr. Schumacher?

HENDERSON • Our mutual friend, Satish Kumar, introduced us over the telephone in the early 1970s. Mr. Kumar is a former Jain monk who now runs Schumacher College in Devon, England, about four hours from London in the middle of the Cornwall peninsula. I often teach there. Dr. Schumacher was assistant editor-in-chief on Satish Kumar's *Resurgence* magazine. I serve on its editorial board.

IKEDA • I believe Dr. Schumacher wrote an article titled "Buddhist Economics" in *Resurgence.*

HENDERSON • Yes. Mr. Kumar telephoned to ask me to arrange lecture dates for Dr. Schumacher, who was planning to go to the United States. Of course, I had read Dr. Schumacher's books and felt great affinity for them. The telephone call from Satish Kumar made it possible to meet him in person and to connect with Robert Swann, who later founded the Schumacher Society in Great Barrington, Massachusetts. That organization is now led by Susan Witt as well as Ian Baldwin, the founder of Chelsea Green Publishing.

IKEDA • Then you got to know each other better.

HENDERSON • Yes. When Fritz Schumacher came to the United States, he stayed at our house in Princeton. With his emphasis on spirituality, he didn't seem like an economist at all. I held a seminar at our home, and people agreed to come meet him as long as no one saw them. The group was small but very important as it included Princeton faculty members and many who worked with me on global issues.

IKEDA • Your decision to hold meetings like that exemplifies your wisdom. Under such circumstances, prejudice and suspicion are relaxed. Everyone meets face to face in a family atmosphere. This is in keeping with Dr. Schumacher's ideas on the abuses to which large organizations are susceptible.

HENDERSON • Yes. Dr. Schumacher stayed with us often in our Princeton house, which I named The Princeton Center for Alternative Futures. He was perfectly willing to help with the chores as part of the small seminars I convened — just a very down-to-earth, ordinary person.

One event I helped Robert Swann organize for him in 1973 was a visit to the Ford Foundation. Mr. Swann, himself a dedicated economic reformer, insisted Dr. Schumacher should talk to the top people at Ford. Only three people showed up. They were so elitist and out of touch. I organized a lunch with Wall Street experts who showed a similar lack of interest. Later, they were amazed when an event was organized for Dr. Schumacher at San Francisco's Cow Palace, and he filled that entire sports stadium.

IKEDA • The elitists didn't want to understand his real value until they had some clear proof of how wonderful he was.

HENDERSON • Yes. When Dr. Schumacher's *Small Is Beautiful* became a bestseller, he was invited to the White House to meet President Jimmy Carter, and I helped arrange a lunch in the U.S. Senate dining room. It's vital to treat everyone the same and to speak with an open heart.

IKEDA • That is the first premise of dialogue. What influence did Dr. Schumacher exert on you?

The importance of humility

HENDERSON • One of the things I learned from him was the importance of operating in a humble situation; that is, you don't have to be powerful in the ordinary sense to be effective. In fact, he used to say that his best learning experience had been when he was imprisoned in Britain. As a German, he was in an internment camp during World War II. He had to live in a camp in a room with about twenty people. All of them worked in the fields every day. They were all from different walks of life. He called this experience the best way to learn to operate in a very humble situation and to be strong in spite of everything.

IKEDA • How people live in adverse circumstances reveals their real value. Josei Toda became enlightened to the true nature of life and awakened to his own mission while in prison. Dr. Schumacher turned his trials into energy. Truly great people not only retain but also elevate their selfhood even in concentration camps and prisons. Mahatma Gandhi and Nelson Mandela are good examples. As is well known, Jawaharlal Nehru wrote extensively in prison. During his fifth and sixth incarcerations, he wrote letters teaching his beloved daughter history. During his ninth time in jail, he wrote *Discovering India.*

Openly opposed to the Japanese militarists of his time, Josei Toda was thrown into prison with Tsunesaburo Makiguchi. Although it ruined his health, he later said that for the sake of his beliefs he was willing to go to prison again. "After a couple of years in prison, you will no longer be scared by anything," he said. "If it's for the sake of Buddhism, I'm ready to go back to prison."

HENDERSON • Mr. Toda was very resolute. Dr. Schumacher's attitude toward lifestyle was another thing that impressed me. He would say that it's very good to live quietly because then nobody notices what you're doing. He had a farm in the south of England, ground his own flour, and grew in his garden a lot of the food he ate.

He was a whole human being. He understood about soil and founded The Soil Association. He understood that good soil is the foundation of a good society. The moment that the quality of the soil is spoiled, civilization goes down the tube.

IKEDA • What he learned from actual daily life was firm and sound. He knew from experience the place of human life within the ecological system.

HENDERSON • He truly deserved respect. Dr. Schumacher and I often enjoyed giving lectures together. We were deep allies, and I was devastated when he died — on his way to another lecture in Switzerland in 1977. I feel I am carrying a banner for him in the struggle for peace, justice and ecological sanity. He was also a spiritual guide to me.

Since I moved to St. Augustine, Florida, in 1986, I have convened many small seminars like the ones Dr. Schumacher took part in. I met my life partner, mathematician Alan F. Kay, at a similar meeting. We married in 1996.

IKEDA • Destiny is inscrutable. Did you move to St. Augustine because of its beautiful environment?

HENDERSON • Yes. Dr. Schumacher is part of the reason I live there. As I said, he maintained that it is good to live quietly because then nobody notices what you're doing. One reason I love living there is that people discount me. They say, "She doesn't live in New York or Boston or California, so is she retired?" If you attract a lot of unwelcome attention, it doesn't help you, does it? I never wanted to be famous, because I knew it would be a lot of trouble. It would draw a lot of fire, because people find something to object to if you're well known.

IKEDA • I understand how you feel. Instead of pursuing fame and position, it is better to live your own way, following your own faith.

HENDERSON • Indeed.

Leaping specialist walls

HENDERSON • It was through my work on Dr. Schumacher's U.S. lecture tour in 1973 that I got involved with Austrian physicist Fritjof Capra.

IKEDA • Whose book *The Tao of Physics* brought you close to tears.

HENDERSON • Every time I take the book up, I remember the synchronicity: I had just finished reading it when the phone rang and a voice said, "This is Fritjof Capra!" I was bowled over. After all, I had just been thinking of how to find this man and talk to him when all of a sudden he is talking to me on the phone.

He said, "I have been sitting in London with E. F. Schumacher, your friend, and he said that I should contact you to help me write my next book, *The Turning Point.*"

I was the happiest person in the world, because I could not imagine a better collaborator than Capra. He could teach me physics, and I could teach him what I knew about economics and what's wrong with it.

IKEDA • Scholars thoroughly versed in one field tend to be uninformed about others. Studying with people from other areas opens their eyes and expands their possibilities. Often the overlapping of fields of interest stimulates new themes. Capra's

The Turning Point, a revision of his earlier work, strongly encourages a paradigm shift for society as a whole.

In reference to your own words, the last chapter is called "The Way to the Age of the Sun." The following passage seems to epitomize your point of view: "Conventional economists, whether neoclassical, Marxist, Keynesian, or post-Keynesian, generally lack an ecological perspective. Economists tend to dissociate the economy from the ecological fabric in which it is embedded, and to describe it in terms of simplistic and highly unrealistic theoretical models. Most of their basic concepts, narrowly defined and used without the pertinent ecological context, are no longer appropriate for mapping economic activities in a fundamentally interdependent world."

HENDERSON • I also learned a lot from Capra. In the years to come, the interdisciplinary approach is going to be indispensable to all kinds of research. As I always say, the ideal is the whole human being. People, particularly in the media, want to say, "She's an economist." I didn't want to have any of those identities. I wanted to be a whole human being. The moment the media gets the idea that you're an economist or a futurist or whatever, you lose the whole of who you are. I thought it would be much better to fly below the media's radar.

The modern world is vertically divided into fields of specialization like economics, sociology, physics, engineering and psychology. But I feel we should break free of these limited categories. These fragmented fields of learning should be fertilizer for the cultivation of a new, holistic view of the world.

IKEDA • I agree entirely. Your ideas correspond with Buddhist thought. As you point out, modern scholarship is so specialized and compartmentalized that much research loses sight of the overall view. This causes trouble. In the past, all learning was called philosophy, and it originated in human life. Learning must serve the good of humanity. This is why we must do our utmost to reinstate a philosophy based on an all-embracing view.

HENDERSON • For me, Capra's *Turning Point* is an attempt to do just that. I am also doing cooperative research with many other scholars, including David Loye, Riane Eisler and the General Evolution Research Group's Darwin Project, to teach David Loye's book *Darwin's Lost Theory of Love.*[2] It strengthens my own work to collaborate in publishing the results of their works and that of many others as well. Through cooperative research of this kind, we can discover a philosophy and a new technology for protecting earth's environment. At the same time, we can form a global culture.

I am confident that this dialogue with you is an important challenge for the creation of an all-encompassing philosophy and a new global culture.

FIVE

Thinking Globally, Acting Locally

IKEDA • You, as a mother, started a wave of changes and have inspired the world. You surely encouraged women greatly, and I hope there will be many to follow in your footsteps.

HENDERSON • Thank you. I am pleased to see my experiences help others.

IKEDA • Who originated the now famous slogan "Think globally, act locally"? You helped popularize it, and then the Club of Rome picked it up.

HENDERSON • It was the French scientist René Dubos, a pioneer of environmental issues. All I did was to popularize it, because I thought it was so fitting. He contributed to the book *Who Speaks for the Earth?*, edited by Barbara Ward and Maurice Strong for the UN Environmental Summit in Stockholm in 1972. I first met Dr. Dubos at the conference.

IKEDA • A world authority in bacteriology, René Dubos is also a critic of civilization from the ecological viewpoint. I met him and his wife in Tokyo in November 1973. Whenever the conversation turned to the environment, his ordinarily gentle expression became very serious and he said things like, "Our approach to the environment must be, not materialistic, but humane."

When I told him of my standing hope that the twenty-first would be a Century of Life, he smiled and nodded in agreement. He was another of the people with whom Arnold Toynbee recommended I meet and talk.

Getting to Stockholm

HENDERSON • One association leads to another. In this case, Barbara Ward introduced me to Dr. Dubos. She was a famous British economist who held a chair at Columbia University. At the time, 1972, I was lucky enough to be a member of a Columbia University faculty committee on technology and social change. She was on that faculty. She invited me to be involved in the process of preparing background material for the UN Environmental Summit.

IKEDA • That Stockholm summit was the first major step toward solving the world's environmental problems.

HENDERSON • Correct. But when the time for it arrived, I didn't have the money to go. At that point, my husband and I were quite poor because journalists don't make much money. Still I had decided that my life depended on getting to Stockholm. So, remembering that I, too, was a journalist — one who had published several articles in the *Harvard Business Review* — I found a small publisher and offered to cover the Stockholm conference for them. They agreed to pay my fare and $500.

IKEDA • You were both enthusiastic and resourceful.

HENDERSON • It's just that I was eager to take part for the first time in a historic international conference debating global environmental issues. I came into contact with the ideas of many people and made many new friends. I'm deeply grateful to Barbara Ward for giving me the opportunity. She had as much an influence on me as E. F. Schumacher had.

IKEDA • When did you first meet her?

HENDERSON • I had an opportunity to get to know her about five years before I met Dr. Schumacher. A quintessential planetary citizen, she wrote *Spaceship Earth* in 1964. I especially related to her habit of considering both the rich and the poor. As an economist, she made it perfectly clear that poverty gaps were the result of bad economics. There is absolutely no need for them. She impressed me enormously. She remained a friend and wrote a nice comment on the jacket of my first book. She did a lot of work with the United Nations — another connection between us.

Although she died about twenty years ago, the copy she gave me of Aldous Huxley's *The Perennial Wisdom* is still one of my treasures. She always had it at her bedside, and now it's at mine.

IKEDA • You cherished an unchanging friendship and worked for the same goals. You called her a quintessential planetary citizen. You yourself are another. What are some of the important points for living as a planetary citizen?

HENDERSON • It's not hard to become a planetary citizen. Because of the development of the media, it's easy to learn about the problems of the planet earth. You can get an immediate grasp of issues like environmental pollution, poverty and hunger from television and the other media. Then, with an awareness of yourself as a world citizen and of the responsibility this entails, you do the best you can in your local area to stimulate action to cope with those problems. This is the spirit embodied in René Dubos's slogan: "Think globally, act locally."

No matter where you are, you'll find problems related to you. This is how I started the drive to clean up the New York environment. Then I came to see that many local problems are related to world problems. It's possible to think on a global scale and act in your own region.

IKEDA • Instead of being bound in narrow frameworks of national or ethnic groups, we must expand our range of vision to the whole world and to all humanity. This is thinking globally.

At the same time, we must keep a firm foothold in the place where we live and persevere in methodical action aimed at bettering society.

With this combined approach, without lapsing into narrow-minded self-righteousness, movements can generate a driving force for reform. I believe that the SGI peace movement is in harmony with the approach indicated by that slogan. The book *Jinsei Chirigaku* (The Geography of Human Life), written a century ago by Tsunesaburo Makiguchi, provides our movement with a philosophical foundation in keeping with your own ideas.

Mr. Makiguchi taught the importance of realizing that the individual human being is more than just a citizen of a nation-state. We are all members of our local regions and, at the same time, citizens of the whole world.

HENDERSON • In other words, individual identity is improved and refined through complex and open association.

IKEDA • Exactly. With firm footings in both the local region and the world at large, without being swept away by the evils of the nation-state, a person can deepen mutual understanding and promote common happiness and prosperity by being a good neighbor and a good citizen both at home and on the international scene.

Mr. Makiguchi further emphasized the importance of elevating our perspective by seeing the local region from the standpoint of the world and the world from the standpoint of the local region. Through this back-and-forth process, future topics of importance become apparent.

The light and dark of globalization

HENDERSON • I'm surprised to learn that Mr. Makiguchi advanced this philosophy a century ago. You just spoke of being more than a member of a state and of being citizens of the world. That is precisely the course I am trying to follow. "Think globally, act locally" epitomizes my philosophy. Yet today, we must act globally, too.

IKEDA • Speaking of globalization, the protest movement against the World Trade Organization was big news.

HENDERSON • Yes, the famous "Battle of Seattle" challenged the "economism" of the WTO's narrow free-trade goals — set largely by big corporations. Today, global-citizen movements have organized the World Social Forum and produced brilliant WTO critiques, setting forth saner approaches to human development, social justice and ecological sustainability. The International Forum on Globalization had opposed economic and technical globalization in favor of decentralization and localization. They now embrace many of the positive policies for reshaping globalization that I have advocated.

I try to listen to the people who categorically deny the possibility of being a planetary citizen or thinking globally. I realize a lot of people think this way. But I'm not sure their way of living and thinking is either desirable or practical.

IKEDA • I understand your doubts. To a certain extent, globalization is inevitable. The point is how to use this change for world peace and human happiness. But in what ways do those with such perspectives react?

HENDERSON • Some of them reject television — which I agree is a degrading influence in that it promotes materialism, consumerism and violence. For example, Jerry Mander, the author of *Four Arguments for the Elimination of Television,* heads the International Forum on Globalization and funds it from his Foundation for Deep Ecology. I met Jerry in Stockholm at the UN Environmental Summit in 1972. He was president of the advertising agency Freeman, Mander & Gossage. He changed his life admirably and, like so many people who reform their lives, did a complete about-face. His book is insightful; but let's face it, how would societies repeal television, radio, satellites, computers or the Internet? We need to reform television and bring technological choices with such huge social impacts under public scrutiny, as the U.S. Congress Office of Technology Assessment did from 1974 until 1996, when corporations lobbied Congress and got it shut down. Now antiglobalization groups use radio and the Internet to oppose economic globalization. Some also use the Internet to organize teach-ins emphasizing the impossibility of being global, or planetary, citizens.

Happily, a more positive agenda for globalizing human rights, workplace standards and environmental protection emerged at the first World Social Forum, where civic leaders met in Porto Alegre, Brazil, in 2001. Some sixty thousand nongovernmental organizations met there again in February 2002, and more than one hundred thousand in 2003. The 2004 meeting was in Mumbai, India.

IKEDA • The World Social Forum was widely publicized in Japan. The focus of the forum was poverty and how to rectify the negative aspects of globalization. I, too, think we should listen to the voices of the suffering people and help them so that we can solve problems without delay and from the global standpoint.

In my 2001 peace proposal, I made an appeal to establish, within the frame of international cooperation, a forum to deliberate on an equitable human-centered global society. The World Social Forum really caught my attention.

The new isolationism

HENDERSON • We cannot think only in terms of local regions and the village. The question is not *whether* to globalize but *what* to globalize. Clearly we must not globalize everything. We can't globalize all of the bad economics now destroying much of our planet. But we do want to globalize ethics; corporate codes of conduct; agreements and treaties to protect human rights. We want to raise workplace standards and conserve our environment.

In the 1960s in New York City, it was clear that everybody requires clean air to breathe, wherever they are. The air moves over the whole planet. I still believe that everybody has the capacity to grasp the interconnections. The idea that we're not smart enough is ridiculous. We use only 10 percent of our brain's capacity, thereby underestimating our human potential to grow in planetary awareness.

I am most interested in your work toward responsible global governance and your peace proposals. What do you think of the current debate about globalization?

IKEDA • Before going on to that, I should like to express my agreement with you on humanity's limitless potential. As Norman Cousins — whom you have praised as a model planetary citizen — said, the danger in human life today is not humanity's lack of ability but the insufficient recognition of the existence of human abilities.

The problem with globalization as it is now and as it will be is the nature of the world it strives for. Former UN Secretary-General Boutros Boutros-Ghali told me in 1998 that, in light of the globalization of financial, environmental and health issues, domestic problems cannot be solved without addressing international ones. People must be interested, he said, not only in their own countries but also in international conditions. They feel uneasy when confronted with the tide of internationalization and withdraw into their own small "villages" (region or state) and traditions, tending to avoid encounters with foreigners. He called this a new isolationism.

HENDERSON • I have observed the same tendency. But isolationism is no longer acceptable.

IKEDA • Precisely. At the same time, globalization based on competition exacerbates disparity in wealth and other evils. If it continues as it's going now, it will gravely damage the global environment and repeat in different forms the tragedies inflicted by imperialism and colonialism up through the first half of the twentieth century.

I therefore insist on the need to draw up international rules for globalization and to create a diverse, cooperative, global society. To this end, each individual must change the models of his or her actions.

Things are now operating according to the law of the jungle: the strong get stronger and the weak weaker. If this continues, the gap between rich and poor will expand on a global scale. We must abandon the jungle law and convert to a cooperative awareness in which everyone can be happy and victorious. The model of our actions must be a way of life permitting everyone to create social value so that we can build a just and compassionate global society.

Media welcome

IKEDA • We must pursue ways of using television, the Internet and the other media effectively in keeping with these principles. The media can be good or bad. How human beings use them is the determining factor. To its credit, the information revolution — symbolized by the Internet — has created an environment in which information is available not merely to an elite segment of the population but, to some extent at least, to the masses. In this environment, grassroots-level exchanges of opinion as a part of daily life are possible globally. This kind of interactive openness is a mainstay of democracy.

HENDERSON • I think that is the way the media ought to be, too. I became a writer because I knew the power of the media — not just books and editorials but also television, radio and now the World Wide Web. Effective use of the media is important in expanding a civic movement. That was one reason I was taken by what Norman Cousins was doing with his magazine and why I was fascinated with public broadcasting and became active in supporting New York's Channel 13, the very first U.S. public-broadcasting channel.

Over the last twenty-five years, I have become very interested in television because it is an incredible communications tool and potentially an educational one as well. Television was, I felt, being wasted by overcommercialization. This led to my constant experimentation to find other roles for television and to pursue its possibilities.

IKEDA • What kinds of experiments?

HENDERSON • I produced a TV series at the University of Florida for the Public Broadcasting Service in 1984. Founded in 1969, PBS now has more than three hundred stations.

In the twelve episodes of the series, titled *Creating Alternative Futures*, I interviewed futurists Alvin Toffler, Barbara Marx Hubbard, Jean Houston and Ziauddin Sardar; the economist Lester Thurow; and Fritjof Capra. Later the programs were broadcast in Australia and New Zealand, and Spanish-language versions were prepared for Latin America.

From 1988 until the present, I interviewed many guests on television for the Florida Community College and its Open Campus televised courses, including Ashok Khosla, president of the Society for Development Alternatives, Delhi; Dee Hock, founder of VISA International and author of *Birth of the Chaordic Age*; and other notables.

IKEDA • Lester Thurow supports transformation of the social system that always produces losers and weak people. The ideas he expresses in his book *The Zero-Sum Society* share much in common with your ideas. He has spoken to me of his concern with the inequitable expansion and rich–poor gap inherent in capitalism and with finding ways to overcome them and realize a society of equality and justice.

HENDERSON • I interviewed him on the theme of global economic restructuring. It is essential that each member of the public correctly understand not only economic issues but also all the problems we confront. In our complex industrial society, we must devise ways to use the communications media. In television, delivery of information must not be limited to a few businesses or groups. Today, we need global grassroots public access to television, which is why I'm helping to develop

74

Canada's WETV. The *WE* stands for "We the People" and the "Whole Earth." WETV has now launched the Green Channel in Canada. My current TV project is *Ethical Marketplace*, a financial program covering all the best-managed, cleanest, greenest companies — an alternative to Bloomberg on sustainable economies. An introduction to this series can be found at www.ethicalmarketplace.com.

IKEDA • A very interesting project. I think the media must adopt a global viewpoint and also reflect the voices of the people. The problem is that, in the face of a globalizing world, conceptions of politics, education and the mass media remain unglobalized. The people must realize that they are the ones who must take up the challenge of breaking this deadlock. Cultivating such concepts is one reason behind the exhibitions that the SGI has sponsored on disarmament, the environment and human rights. With its Global Learning program, the United Nations University is working to the same end. But much remains to be done on the part of ordinary people.

Newspapers and dialogue

HENDERSON • The reason I stay in touch with the SGI is because of its grassroots activism on global issues and the dedicated local leaders I meet wherever I go. I was honored to speak at the SGI-USA Women Building Peace Conference at the World Bank in February 2001. More than two thousand people came — a new experience for the World Bank! It was very impressive.

In propagating a message, it is important to move step by step to broaden a sense of solidarity while making effective use of the media. The Soka Gakkai newspaper *Seikyo Shimbun* is certainly successful in this kind of undertaking.

IKEDA • The *Seikyo Shimbun* celebrated its fiftieth anniversary in 2001 and now has a circulation of 5.5 million.

This newspaper began as a result of discussions I shared with Josei Toda. Even while his own business affairs remained up in the air, with an eye on the future, he was mulling over plans to start a periodical. As we sat in a small Tokyo restaurant, he said to me: "Let's start a newspaper. This is the age of free speech, and a newspaper is the prime weapon in the struggle to pioneer free speech."

With these words, the *Seikyo Shimbun* came into being. Now, at home and abroad, it has a high reputation for disseminating a humanistic philosophy devoted to promoting peace, culture and education.

HENDERSON • Mr. Toda was very perceptive. Your many dialogues effectively disseminate your philosophy throughout the world. What led you to make this kind of appeal?

IKEDA • I learned the challenge of dialogue from my mentor. Then, too, Buddhist philosophy is oriented toward dialogue. Mr. Toda's most cherished wish was to eliminate misery from the earth. He taught me that accomplishing this requires meetings and exchanges with people and engaging in dialogues that connect humanity in unbreakable solidarity. His teaching has inspired me to meet and talk with informed people and leaders all over the world.

Among the dialogues, I especially remember the one I was privileged to conduct with Arnold Toynbee. It was highly fruitful because its vast civilizational and religious range extended over millennia of human history. All my dialogue partners have felt sincere responsibility for the future of humanity. Transcending all differences, we have been united in mind by strong spiritual bonds.

HENDERSON • It was in this spirit that you were one of the early people to conduct dialogues in the Soviet Union and China.

IKEDA • Yes, that's true. I believed there were people to talk to in socialist nations, too. So, even during the Cold War, I built bridges of friendship to countries like China and the Soviet Union. Some people criticized me as a man of religion for visiting countries that rejected religion. But I was convinced that people are people in spite of ideological differences. What's more, precisely because of our differences, we must engage in dialogue. This is why I have repeatedly held discussions with people from many different religious, ethnic and cultural backgrounds.

HENDERSON • That's admirable. How did you seek out people with whom you could hold philosophical discussions?

IKEDA • As I have mentioned, acquaintances introduced me to new friends. Mr. Toynbee introduced me to Aurelio Peccei, founder of the Club of Rome. Through Mr. Peccei, I became close with other Club of Rome members. With each encounter, I prized and strove to deepen new friendships. Thanks to this process of expanding friendships, I have now engaged in more than fifteen hundred dialogues. Though perhaps a modest means, dialogue can build bridges and lay roads leading to lasting peace. Such is my unchanging belief.

Revolutionizing Civilization

Peccei leads the way

IKEDA • Thirty years have passed since the Club of Rome's "The Limits to Growth" report created its initial impact. It aroused extensive debate by proposing an annihilation scenario for our race and our planet. As a consequence, a movement to reexamine modern civilization took hold.

I first met Aurelio Peccei in May 1975, three years after the publication of the report. He was kind enough to call on me in Sceaux, in the suburbs of Paris, where I was visiting. Beneath his courteous and affable manner, I sensed his convictions of steel preserved from when he was a young man struggling against the fascists. When I got to know him, he was widely criticized as the prophet of doom. Some claimed his pessimistic forecast failed to take into consideration scientific-technological progress.

The oil-shock that occurred the very next year, however, made them take his warnings more seriously. Thus, "The Limits to Growth" became the first major step toward global concern with environmental problems. No one today denies this. Although many found the report too gloomy, I believe it performed a great service by highlighting the issue from a global viewpoint.

HENDERSON • I agree. "The Limits to Growth" overturned the conventional wisdom that gross national product was an adequate indicator of overall economic growth, since it ignored environmental depletion and pollution. This upset the scholarly world, which tried to bury the epoch-making report.

I admired Dr. Peccei tremendously. He was mayor of Rome when I first met him. His expansive vision impressed me deeply.

IKEDA • His message was that we must recognize the situation confronting us and act before time runs out.

He expressed his affinity with the SGI movement, saying that, ultimately, the reformation of human nature that he had long advocated requires what we in the SGI call the human revolution. Dr. Peccei's pronouncements always reflected his custom of examining issues from the standpoint of the whole human race and his sense of responsibility for future generations. This made an indelible impression on me.

Donella Meadows's village of one hundred people

HENDERSON • Actually I was familiar with its ideas before "The Limits to Growth" was published.

As you know, a group of MIT professors — Jay Forrester, Dennis Meadows and Donella Meadows — were commissioned by the Club of Rome to compile the report. I interviewed this group before the report was issued. Their research was called the Limits to Growth Project. My work with Citizens for Clean Air made me realize that we humans were dealing with a much bigger problem than air pollution. Donella and Dennis Meadows were working with the global problem. My interview with them and Jay Forrester was published in *The Futurist* in 1971. The article introduced the fact that the MIT group was grappling on the global level with pollution, poverty, injustice and everything that we humans must understand if we are going to save ourselves from extinction.

IKEDA • Sadly, Donella Meadows died recently. Her importance is now being re-appreciated. After the terrorist attacks of September 11, 2001, a certain e-mail message circulated all over the world and caused quite a stir. Titled "If the world were a village of one hundred people," this thought-provoking, easy-to-understand analysis, published in book form even in Japan, made a big hit. It was originally written by Donella Meadows.

HENDERSON • Yes. Donella was another of my heroes. Because of my articles concerning her and the other members of the group, Dr. Peccei invited me to attend Limits to Growth meetings in Salzburg in 1973, Caracas, Berlin and again in Salzburg. These meetings produced a report called "No Limits to Learning" in 1979.

Although I never knew Dr. Peccei in a personal way — only in a sort of policy way at the meetings we attended together — I mourned his death, because he was a magnificent human being who saw things very clearly. He was one of those people from the future.

Shifting to higher goals

IKEDA • The former Club of Rome president, Richard Diez-Hochleitner, described Dr. Peccei as a living flame. Certainly a profound concern for humanity and trust in and sense of responsibility for the human race burned bright in his heart. As is well known, though imprisoned and cruelly tortured by fascists during World War II, he never betrayed his comrades. He believed deeply in them and in all humanity. I saw him for the last time in June 1983, nine months before his death. Until the very end, he concerned himself earnestly with the future of humanity. He said that, although our external resources are limited, the inner wealth of humanity is boundless and the process of human revolution is the key to positive action leading to the adoption of a new course and the revival of human fortunes.[1]

HENDERSON • Wonderful words that are all the more interesting because they represent the conclusion of your dialogue with Dr. Peccei. Humanity's current fixation on materialistic, GNP-measured economic growth obscured our higher path toward learning and toward our moral and spiritual growth. Shifting to higher human goals, social equity and quality of life is also the path to environmental sustainability and restoration.

IKEDA • Dr. Peccei and I were of one accord in believing that only a human revolution that reforms our views of the natural world, life and even our values has the power to alter human destiny.

"The Limits to Growth" is more than a warning signal. It inspires courage and hope by pointing out the necessity and the possibility of a fundamental reformation of humanity.

HENDERSON • Only the human revolution can reform our views of the natural world, life and values. We have the power to alter our destiny. This is very much my own view. It is really what my work for the last thirty years has been about.

An economy based on spiritual growth

HENDERSON • As you say, three decades have passed since Dr. Peccei issued his warning; but, far from going away, the crisis is getting worse. How can we break the conventional wisdom that we can drive the economy forward only by destroying the environment and hurting people? One problem with the old way is its assumption that the totally materialistic GNP measures economic growth. We can grow in so many other dimensions. We can grow in wisdom, in intelligence and in knowledge. And we can run a very good economy based on cooperation and spiritual growth.

Happily, scientists have recently proved wrong the core theory of economics: that humans are selfish and compete to maximize their self-interest. Biologists have refuted this in their research on the hormone oxytocin, which is the basis of our ability to trust and bond with one another for mutual support.[2]

IKEDA • Healthy economics based on spiritual development — a highly important concept. In the twentieth century, human influence extended to outer space; but our inner development was shamefully neglected.

HENDERSON • Yes. Now that the economists have been defrocked, we can amplify the cooperative side of human nature. I always like to point to Austria as an example of an economy based on spiritual growth. In the nineteenth century, the Austrian economy depended on music. And the world has been enjoying that Austrian music ever since.

IKEDA • Austria's high-quality "software" of culture to enrich the spirit is a good example of spiritual social abundance.

HENDERSON • And Japan's social solidarity is a good example of a more cooperative economy. Many economists now agree we must abandon the materialistic "hardware" view and "dematerialize" the GNP in the direction of spiritual and intellectual growth. That's what I've been trying to do by means of the Calvert-Henderson Quality of Life Indicators. They are now updated regularly at www.calvert-henderson.com.

These new indicators for the United States honor the unpaid work in society: caring, sharing, volunteering, nurturing others. They measure health, education, human rights, infrastructure, the building of community and valuing and protecting the environment.

IKEDA • That's what you called the "love economy." As you say, changing society means we absolutely must reexamine the basic meaning of affluence and alter the scale by which we measure it.

Changing our scale completely alters the way we see the world. If, as Donella Meadows posited, earth were a village with one hundred inhabitants, 59 percent of its wealth would be in the hands of a mere six people. Only one person would have a college education, and only two would own a computer. Viewing the state of the world in this way clearly reveals the inequalities we must face.

The real "axis of evil"

HENDERSON • Yes, we must rethink our own position and those of the others with whom we share the planet in order to build peace in the world. The real "axis of evil" we must overcome consists of poverty, ignorance, disease and violence.

IKEDA • To continue with the metaphor, twenty of the hundred people in the global village would account for 80 percent of all energy consumption, thereby leaving only 20 percent for the remaining eighty people. Energy, one of our gravest concerns, interrelates with such other issues as the environment, population, food and the gap between the rich and the poor. You've described our current state of affairs in a forthright fashion. In less than three hundred years, humanity will have depleted the fossilized sources of energy — petroleum, coal and natural gas —

that took sixty million years to accumulate.

Data varies as to how much fossil fuel remains. No matter what the figures, however, if we do not change our lifestyles, the mass production, mass consumption and mass disposal endemic to modern civilization will exhaust them all in less than several hundred years.

HENDERSON • Yes, the energy situation is crucial. As a short-term policy, we must improve the efficiency with which we use fossil fuels. We can make power plants more efficient using cogeneration techniques — such as recycling steam that would otherwise be wasted to heat nearby facilities. But, basically, we have to make a switch from fossil fuels. Natural gas is the transition fuel, but it is already becoming scarce. The nuclear and fossil-fuel industries are making a last stand. They are still powerful vested interests.

In many ways, "energy crisis" is a misnomer for what is happening in the United States. There is no real energy crisis here. The critical situation is brought on by our inability to conserve energy. We waste so much energy that, as studies show, improving efficiency would be far less expensive than building more power plants. Yet in 2003, the U.S. Congress produced an energy bill that would hamper such progress and continue subsidizing the fossil-fuel economy and nuclear energy.

IKEDA • Some reports claim that energy efficiency in the United States is less than 10 percent.

Contagious exhaustion

HENDERSON • More efficient automobiles, refrigerators, air conditioners and buildings would be a quick way to achieve results. Laws should be tightened to enforce these changes.

Japan's low-pollution hybrid cars that get more than 50 miles to the gallon are rapidly gaining favor in the U.S. market. It takes three or four years to build a power plant. It would take ten years to get petroleum out of the Arctic National Wildlife Reserve. But new technologies like hybrid cars, combined with legal measures, can take effect much faster.

The falling U.S. dollar may also force U.S. consumers to conserve energy and import less, since the United States is already the world's largest debtor.[3]

IKEDA • From the standpoint of the burden on the environment, increased efficiency is just as important as, or even more important than, energy production. German statesman and Club of Rome member Ernest Ulrich von Weizsäcker has said that our society is the victim of contagious exhaustion. The problem cannot be solved unless we overcome the modern social tendency to waste resources and waste our lives.

HENDERSON • He and his wife, Christine, a biologist, have done outstanding work on energy, climate change and biotechnology issues. I am proud that they wrote a foreword to the German edition of my book *The Politics of the Solar Age*. Individuals as well as large organizations can help save energy and reduce pollution by simply turning up their thermostats in summer, turning them down in winter, and wearing more sweaters.

IKEDA • Conservation not only assists nations in dealing with energy and environmental problems but also helps households make ends meet. In 2001, the British Ministry of the Environment suggested boiling only the amount of water needed — not a kettleful — for each cup of tea or coffee. That would save about 90 seconds of heating each time. Adhering to this policy for a week would save enough energy to light a normal house for a day or operate a television set for twenty-six hours.

In addition to such conservation, we require technological reforms and the application of all our wisdom to improve energy-consumption efficiency. In the past, businesses have regarded environmental considerations as burdens. They can no longer do so.

Japanese consumers seem to like the low-pollution hybrid car you mentioned. This suggests that environmental considerations afford business a big opportunity rather than involving only extra costs.

At one time, nuclear energy was touted as a replacement for petroleum. What are your thoughts on the current situation with nuclear energy?

Nuclear deceit

HENDERSON • The nuclear-energy people are rushing in, advertising that nuclear energy is clean and nonpolluting. They are very deceitful. The storage of radioactive nuclear wastes is reaching crisis proportions. Furthermore, nuclear energy could not compete in price if it were not for the Price-Anderson Act, which was renewed by U.S. President George Bush. It shifts liability for nuclear accidents to U.S. taxpayers.

IKEDA • Three Mile Island and Chernobyl destroyed the myth of nuclear safety, thus inspiring Germany and other nations to steer away from the nuclear option. In Japan, in 1999, two deaths at a uranium processing plant at Tokai-mura in Ibaraki Prefecture put a damper on the building of new nuclear facilities. What's more, no fundamental ways for dealing with nuclear waste have been developed.

HENDERSON • No, they have not. Nor has the question of safety been dealt with adequately. From my point of view, we must continue opposing further development of nuclear energy. It's the wrong technology. It was a hangover from World War II. The nuclear industry persuaded President Eisenhower that nuclear energy would be atoms for peace. They claimed that, in the United States, electricity would become too cheap to bother with metering. Yet nuclear power plants turned out to be the most expensive of all. In California, where energy costs are extremely high, nuclear power can be said to be cheaper. But the long-term costs are still uncounted, and the dangers are unacceptable. If economists ever account properly for long-term costs, it would become apparent that nuclear power is not cheap.

IKEDA • The greatest cost is incurred by dealing with nuclear waste. Although it may save natural resources and reduce global warming, nuclear energy generation entails the danger of long-term radiation pollution. We cannot afford to postpone the search for a fundamental solution to the energy problem.

Loving the sun

IKEDA • Where are we to turn for new energy sources? You advocate a transition from a petroleum age to an age of light and sunshine. What precisely do you mean?

HENDERSON • I wrote about a future solar and hydrogen economy in 1981 in *The Politics of the Solar Age: Alternatives to Economics.* The vision of an age of light inspired me and came from deep in my intuition. Instead of being taught, I had to teach myself about wind power, solar power, hydrogen fuel cells, tidal power, geothermal power and biomass from work at the U.S. Congress Office of Technology Assessment. From my American Indian friends, I learned of their deep knowledge of the sun, the wind, the land, plants and animals and the proper role of humans as part of Nature's creation. I knew that we industrial people would need to re-learn from their ancient wisdom.

IKEDA • Perhaps your idea of an age of light and sunshine can be summarized in this way: Fossil fuels stored in the earth from the very remote past will be exhausted in the next several hundred years. To deal with this, we must shift from a society that wastes those fuels to a society based on renewable energy sources. Until now human culture has striven to be independent of nature. It must now seriously recognize the mutual connections between humanity and nature. We must return to the ancient appreciation of the earth as the Great Mother. There is much to learn from the past, including equality and cooperation between the sexes. You insist on a necessary paradigm shift or transition to an age of true symbiosis.

HENDERSON • Yes. I love the sun because it is the source of all life. Plants couldn't grow without it. In our discussions, technologists at the Office of Technology Assessment often asked me, "What percentage of the heat for your house can come from solar energy?" I would reply that, if the sun did not pre-heat the house, its temperature would be −400 degrees Fahrenheit.

IKEDA • Warmth does indeed begin with the sun. Furthermore, petroleum and natural gas are, in effect, stored solar energy from the distant past.

HENDERSON • The sun is the mother star for the earth and, without it, nothing can survive even one day — it is really the Mother Sun. This metaphor is directly understandable to ordinary people, but academics cloud it with their wrong theories. From my reading of Soka Gakkai history, I learn that your founder, Mr. Makiguchi, taught that false theories and doctrines could lead the people astray.

IKEDA • Yes, he did. Wrong ideas fundamentally warp society. He therefore taught that, to change society, we must rectify our way of thinking. Nichiren's ideas about the relationship between a correct teaching and a peaceful land provide a philosophical foundation for us. Mr. Makiguchi argued that mistaken Shinto thought was driving Japan to war and destruction. For saying such things, the authorities, who were leading the nation into militarism, threw him into prison, where he subsequently died.

Our primary emphasis — education founded on true humanism — arises from that history. As education brings out the good aspects of humanity and society, it can also bring out the bad aspects.

But, to return to the energy issue, you enumerate several possible alternative sources: wind power, solar power, hydrogen, fuel cells, tidal power, geothermal power and biomass. Which of them is most promising?

HENDERSON • I believe that hydrogen — made using solar and wind power— and other renewable energy sources will become the preferred fuels for transportation and other sectors in the future.

High hopes for hydrogen

IKEDA • Surely many people have high hopes for hydrogen fuel cells, just as for solar cells, which, put simply, employ the chemical reaction between hydrogen and oxygen to generate electricity — clean electrical devices. All of the many types of these cells produce nothing but water as a waste product. In other words, they arouse no concern over the carbon dioxide that is a contributing factor in global warming. The process involved is the reverse of the high-school chemistry experiment that runs an electric current through water to produce hydrogen and oxygen.

The idea is not new. The nineteenth-century English physicist Sir William Robert Grove discovered it in 1839, before electricity was put to use. U.S. researchers studied it seriously in the 1960s in connection with developing electrical source devices for satellites.

Now it is being applied in many parts of the world in automobile engines, domestic electric generators, heaters, water heaters and many other areas. Blessed with plenty of geothermal and water power, Iceland claims that it will shift to hydrogen and reduce consumption of fossil fuels like petroleum and coal to zero in the next twenty or thirty years.

Japan began testing an auto equipped with a hydrogen cell on public roads. It aims, within a few years, to put the auto to practical use. At present, cost and safety problems connected with cell systems and with hydrogen supply persist.

HENDERSON • The introduction of hydrogen fuel cells will occur as soon as countries find the political will to stop subsidizing fossil-fuel and nuclear industries. In the United States, the Bush administration now supports hydrogen but still also subsidizes coal, oil and nuclear. In many other countries, these industries finance political campaigns and so still have a stranglehold on governments.

IKEDA • For better or worse, the energy problem to a large extent depends on political will, which in turn is driven by popular will. We must scrupulously investigate whether politics is directed toward the benefit of local people, the peoples of the world and future generations or toward the interests of specific industries. Apparently government leaders in some countries are rapidly introducing things like solar- and wind-powered generators. Which are most successful at implementing programs of renewable energy?

Endowment and enlightenment

HENDERSON • Those countries with the best natural endowments and the best policies — Denmark, Germany, the Netherlands, Britain and Portugal — employ wind power.

IKEDA • I understand that Poul La Cour, who is known as the Danish Edison, began using wind energy to generate electricity as early as 1891. The Swedish, too, use generators powered entirely by the wind.

HENDERSON • Lester Brown, founder of Worldwatch Institute, says in *Eco-Economy: Building an Economy for the Earth* that the Midwestern United States could potentially harness as much energy from the wind as from OPEC's oil.

IKEDA • In Japan, on Hokkaido and elsewhere, wind-power generators are increasingly popular.

HENDERSON • Beside wind power, the Brazilians also use both solar power and hydropower. There are many solar-powered facilities in Florida, but the state is still dominated by the fossil-fuel and nuclear industries. Maine has the possibility of huge tidal power, the use of which Presidents John F. Kennedy and Franklin D. Roosevelt advocated. Ocean currents in many parts of the world can also be harnessed with underwater turbines to produce electrical power with less impact than dams. But it is not enough for a country to have good natural endowments; it must also have highly enlightened policies. With those two things together, the transition can happen.

IKEDA • I agree entirely. In global capitalism, minimum government is considered best. The issue, however, is not the extent of a government but its vision.

Fluctuations in petroleum prices seem to control the will to conserve energy and develop new sources.

HENDERSON • Yes. The fact that Saudi Arabia and the countries of the Middle East have too much oil for their own good proved to be a minus. Because oil was cheap and easy to get at, they never did anything about their enormous potential for solar energy. Oil became a substitute for thought. Because of its dearth of natural resources, Japan has developed less wasteful, more efficient technologies.

IKEDA • That's true. Japan consistently occupies a high rank among the industrialized nations for energy-use efficiency and for industrial-waste recycling.

To the concern of many, the United States withdrew from the Kyoto Accord, which attempts to regulate carbon-dioxide emissions.

HENDERSON • Yes, very regrettably. It is most encouraging, however, as I read in a recent UN report, even after the United States and subsequently Russia pulled out of the Kyoto Accord, the other signatory nations went straight ahead promoting solar and renewable energy. They realize that whether the United States and Russia join in or not is immaterial. Greater energy efficiency and sustainability are good ideas for all of them, even if some countries don't yet understand this. So I think that Europe will begin to move faster. Already, the giant insurance company Swiss Re has committed to reducing its carbon emissions, as have other companies. The idea is certainly alive with the new government of President "Lula" da Silva in Brazil, where I have been active, as well as in other Latin American countries and in Australia. There is a "green" government in New Zealand now headed by Prime Minister Helen Clark. President Chen Shuei Bian of Taiwan envisions his country as the "Green Silicon Island."

IKEDA • Each country should implement such good ideas. They should set an example for countries where protecting industry is considered more important than protecting the environment and try to find clues for policy changes. This becomes even more important when we remember that we are racing against time.

HENDERSON • Subsidies are the key for transitioning to clean energy in each nation. Annually some trillion dollars in perverse subsidies go to encourage the use of coal, oil, nuclear energy and wasteful industries and infrastructure. It may be unnecessary to subsidize new energy sources if the subsidies for old ones were eliminated, as they should certainly be! This would permit new technologies to compete on a level playing field. In some cases, subsidies as well as investments will be needed to kick-start developments in hydrogen, fuel cells and solar energy. Wind power, on the other hand, is already fully competitive and steadily growing more popular.

The tax shift

IKEDA • Once, when you were asked what policies you would adopt if you were president, after mentioning education, you said you would revise the tax system to cut subsidies for old-energy industries.

HENDERSON • Yes, tax shifting is very important. Right now we tax all the wrong things. We grant oil companies depletion *allowances* when we should impose depletion *taxes.* Our current course is completely backward. The tax shift I've been promoting for many years would remove the tax from incomes and payrolls: we want full employment. The government's overall revenues would remain unchanged, but taxes would be imposed on the use and waste of natural resources. This would correct pricing because adding costs to prices would ensure that heavily polluting products are more expensive. So consumers would buy fewer polluting products. I have advocated such "green" taxes since 1989, pointing to the example of Europe.

IKEDA • A very good idea. Remove inappropriate subsidies and the tax shift would become a mainstay in efforts to reform society from a wasteful to a circulative model. Europe is taking the lead in the tax shift. Denmark, Finland, Italy, the Netherlands, Norway and Sweden already impose a so-called carbon tax on carbon-dioxide emissions.

It is said that a nation's society finds expression in its tax system. In the past, tax systems in various countries have put too little emphasis on caring for the environment and too heavy a burden on taxing payrolls and incomes.

HENDERSON • Another policy that would speed things along is for joint ventures to implement green technologies. For example, my Chinese colleagues are working on many levels to license cleaner green technologies. Helping them succeed quickly would be to everybody's advantage. China is in fact making environmental management and energy efficiency pillars of their new economy. The city of Shanghai is spending $2 billion to clean up pollution.

IKEDA • That's very encouraging. I understand that in recent efforts to make China the "Recycling Plant of the World," the government has designated five cities, including Tianjin and Shanghai, as recycling cities and plans to integrate its recycling plants.

We must look upon solving the environmental and energy problems not as a burden but as a frontier challenge as we embark on building a civilization of harmonious symbiosis between human beings and nature and among human beings.

The economist Lester Thurow, whom we have discussed, says that economic growth and protection of the environment are consistent. He adds that technology, far from being a threat to the environment, can actually save it.

SEVEN

A Technology
To Benefit the Future

IKEDA • Among your many written works is an amusing forecast of the future that you co-authored with your grandson. The book is set in the year 2050 when Brendan, who would then be sixty, is living in Shanghai. He writes a letter to you describing how environmental problems have been solved to the extent that Shanghai has a clear blue sky.

"Imagine"

HENDERSON • Yes. Actually, it's an essay included among forty in a book called *Imagine*, edited by Marianne Williamson. It deals with the nature of the world in fifty years. Brendan and I discussed it on the phone. He's very concerned about all the same things that interest me. Since probably I won't be alive in 2050, in the story I am supposed to have died in 2023. He writes a letter addressed to me in memory of our many conversations.

IKEDA • You showed me a photograph of him the last time we met. I understand that he enthusiastically shares your interest in the world. We will expect much from him in the future.

HENDERSON • Thank you. We must make sure the world is a better place when Brendan and his generation grow up. My reason for writing that essay with him was to give people a clear, concrete vision of how things can work. We need a plausible story about how we get from here to there. I found it very effective to use the positive alternatives demonstrated in our essay.

IKEDA • Discussions of the environment tend to sound pessimistic. But, while severely critical of current politico-economics, you never lose your optimism.

HENDERSON • *The New Scientist*, published in London, in a special issue detailed three scenarios of absolute disaster — global warming, pollution and exhausted food supplies. Futurists use gloomy scenarios because of the great uncertainty facing us and because human action is always the key to change. But I got tired of negative scenarios, which sometimes frighten people so much that they don't know what to do. That's why I like to promote positive outlooks, even though I am always aware of negative aspects.

I believe my optimism is an expression of the life force and spirit that every human being and all life share.

The person who believes

IKEDA • A very significant observation. The economist John Kenneth Galbraith has said that those who believe they can do something pure and good for the world make more resolute effort than those who do not. His conviction is that positive, constructive citizens must be optimistic, enthusiastic, outgoing and dynamic.

I would add that nothing great can be accomplished unless leaders combine coolheaded intelligence with passion. You have all these qualifications in abundance. Brendan is lucky to have such a splendid grandmother.

HENDERSON • Why, thank you. Brendan is a lively, curious and loving boy. I'm proud of my daughter and son-in-law for parenting him so well. They live far from me, so mostly I talk to Brendan on the phone and send him books and magazines that cover planetary environmental themes — for instance, *The Dolphin Log*, published by the Cousteau Society.

Brendan tells me schools today include environment in their curricula. When I take walks with him, we clear away cans and litter along our path. I love answering all his questions about the planet and nature.

IKEDA • What a heartwarming picture. Within ordinary daily life, it is crucial to teach young people the importance of loving nature and of being compassionate toward the force of life. Children learn relations with nature and the environment by copying their parents' actions.

I'm sure you teach Brendan about the environment from many different vantage points. After all, it is a very broad and complex subject involving global warming, deforestation, population growth, reduction and pollution of aquifers, and extinction of plant and animal species.

HENDERSON • All the issues you mention can sow the seeds of planetary destruction. Human population growth will stabilize only when women have full human rights, access to education and economic empowerment. Wherever women have gained these rights, birth rates fall.

First understand your differences and then unite

IKEDA • Undeniably, improving the social position of women is an important key to resolving environmental problems. Problems of the environment include many aspects — politics, economics, education, human-rights awareness, ethics, human-value criteria, lifestyles and the nature of society itself. Your contribution has been truly great because you have worked to see that women's voices are heard and that the new current of the times is plotted from the woman's standpoint. Specifically what lessons have you learned?

HENDERSON • I think the most important thing I learned is how to build coalitions. This is particularly true in the environmental movement. I started off with Citizens for Clean Air. Then there were many other groups with names like Citizens for Noise Control, Citizens to Stop Water Pollution, Citizens to Stop Airport Noise, and Citizens for Stopping Pesticides. In 1969, we all came together for the First National Congress on Population and Environment. By meeting together, all the little groups expanded their awareness of being part of an environmental movement. Instead of arguing about who should get funding or the relative importance of specific issues, we saw that we had to form a coalition. All the groups started changing their names to include the word *environment*. Learning how to form a coalition made expanding our movement so much easier.

IKEDA • A vital point. The important thing for groups is not to ignore minor differences in the name of larger issues but to understand minor differences and unite in spite of them. Saving the earth is the big issue. In a sense, who saves it is secondary. In this spirit and in the name of peace and morality, I have engaged in discussions with representatives of many faiths and philosophies — Christianity, Islam, Judaism, Hinduism and communism.

HENDERSON • There are different roles for different souls, and everybody has a distinct personality or way of dealing with life's challenges. Whatever your karma, you must respect it and realize that you are part of a great continuum.

IKEDA • Buddhism illustrates this with the idea that a beautiful garden of happiness and peaceful coexistence is possible if all the trees in it — the cherry, the plum, the peach and the damson — manifest their individualities fully instead of being jealous and emulative of one another. In this sense, manifesting individuality within an awareness of coalition and recognizing the individuality of all other members of the coalition are extremely important points.

HENDERSON • I like to call the solidarity I referred to previously the Ecology of Social Change. Everybody fits in somewhere. We should honor the efforts of anybody who is moving in the right direction, that is, protecting the environment and our children's future. We mustn't find fault with their actions. Often people in groups fail to learn this lesson and criticize one another on petty issues instead of criticizing the polluting organization. As we know, the first law of ecology is that everything is connected to everything else. Buddhism preaches a similar principle, right?

IKEDA • Yes. This is the Buddhist law of dependent origination. Everything arises because of its relationship with other beings or phenomena, and all things exist in mutual relationships.

Ice-free Arctic summers?

IKEDA • Today it is even clearer that nothing that happens anywhere on earth is unrelated to us. Global warming is a classic example. According to a report by the Intergovernmental Panel on Climate Change, by the year 2100, average temperatures will have risen by 1.4 to 5.8 degrees Celsius. The magnitude of the change becomes immediately apparent when we note that, over the past century, temperatures have risen only by about 0.6 of a degree. The Arctic icecap has already been reduced by 40 percent from what it was in the 1950s. One researcher has said that, if this trend goes unchecked, by 2050, Arctic summers will be ice-free. By 2100, sea levels may rise by a maximum of about a meter. Many of the estimated one billion people now living in low-lying areas at or only a few meters above sea level will suffer major hardships. Global warming will drive many animal species to higher ground; many are predicted to become extinct. Insect damage is forecast to worsen, forests will be lost, and coral reefs will whiten in death.

HENDERSON • I am extremely interested to observe that vastly increased claims related to weather damage are compelling European insurance companies to address the issue of carbon-dioxide buildup. At the Office of Technology Assessment, we learned that the first indication of climate change is not necessarily global warming but weather variability. We see this now in freak storms, droughts, heat waves and floods all over the world.

IKEDA • Yes, the 0.6 of a degree that temperatures rose in the past hundred years is barely perceptible. Still, little by little, warming is changing the weather. To give an example, the Japanese cherry tree called the Somei-yoshino starts blooming five days earlier on average than it did fifty years ago.

HENDERSON • The global effect is climate change. In some places it's going to be warmer; in some places, colder. Some areas will be wetter; and in some places new deserts will form as it gets drier.

Hot money and global warming

IKEDA • Some scientists suggest that as melting glaciers alter currents in the Gulf of Mexico, Europe will experience a new Ice Age. In fact, environmental archaeologists suggest that climate change may have been the major factor in the downfall of the ancient civilizations of Egypt, Mesopotamia, the Indus Valley and the Yangtze River Valley.

The German author Michael Ende aptly called the environmental-destruction issue a battle with time. It is not a struggle for territory but a battle threatening ruin for our children and grandchildren. Material civilization squanders our heritage of fossil fuels and sacrifices future generations in the arrogant pursuit of present prosperity. We must put a halt to this trend as fast as possible.

HENDERSON • Yes. Our bankrupt economic paradigm (the social system that gives priority to monetary gains) accelerates global destruction. Global trading of currencies has reached $1.5 trillion every day. Most of this is speculation. Additional flows of hot money (short-term investments and profit seeking) now supercede all other values. This is why I am helping to promote local and electronic bartering systems, without the need for money. My partner, Alan Kay, and I have also designed a currency-trading system that can reduce speculation and allow the collection of a tax. This is the Foreign Exchange Transaction Reporting System.[1]

IKEDA • It's interesting how — thanks to the popularity of Internet commercial transactions, especially among the young — information technology seems to be reviving the ancient barter system.

Choosing global good

IKEDA • To return to the global warming issue, how can we help in practical everyday ways?

HENDERSON • The main thing is to reduce consumption of fossil energy and material goods. In this task, we all fit somewhere in the continuum, and in shifting our life patterns toward personal development, community services and "de-materializing" the GNP from goods toward services and the quality of life.

IKEDA • If repeated often enough, even small personal efforts can save regions, nations and the whole world.

HENDERSON • People might think I live an upscale lifestyle. I travel a lot by plane to give speeches. I entertain a lot of people from other countries in a big house.

Still, we conserve. Our house is big, but we keep energy consumption down by using only compact fluorescent lamps, so energy consumption in the house — even with our offices and computers, faxes and so on — is minimized. I hadn't owned a car since 1986 until we recently bought the Toyota hybrid electric. I much prefer to ride my bicycle. My lifestyle may not be perfect, but I do buy secondhand clothes and furniture out of a dislike for supporting the manufacture of new ones. Whenever we buy secondhand goods, we contribute to environmental preservation. The U.S. economy is still driven by consumption, which accounts for two-thirds of the GDP. People are now questioning this shop-till-you-drop economy and countering it with "Buy Nothing Days" organized by the magazine *Ad Busters* published in Vancouver, Canada.

IKEDA • In Japan, the production, transportation and disposal of daily-life articles account for a significant amount of carbon

104

dioxide emissions that are a major factor in climatic warming. Directly or indirectly, about half of Japan's carbon dioxide emissions are said to be related to domestic life. This being the case, even small changes in daily habits can make a big difference.

HENDERSON • Recycling is also a good way to help the environment. So is bartering. Any time we can reduce the power the money system exerts over our lives, we are helping to save the environment. People rarely think of barter in this connection. But a friend of mine in London — an SGI member in the United Kingdom — operates a nonprofit electronic barter company called Via3.net. We are partners in Via3, helping multiply the resources and effectiveness of local and global NGOs through cooperative exchanges. Of course, in addition to private measures, we must engage in political activities, too.

IKEDA • Official steps are being taken in many countries to promote recycling. In the European Union, manufacturers of electrical appliances and electronic devices are responsible for the collection and disposal of discards.

The take-back trend

HENDERSON • This is a very interesting and important trend. The United States should be implementing this important system, too. Even though the U.S. government is reluctant, many companies, like Hewlett-Packard and Interface, Inc., the commercial carpeting manufacturer, have found that take-back programs save money and are often profitable.

IKEDA • Over the past few years, the Japanese government has passed several laws related to recycling containers, domestic electrical appliances and foodstuffs as well as revisions to legislation promoting effective use of resources. In 2002, a law on construction recycling was adopted and a bill on automobile recycling has been presented. Beginning in April 2001, manufacturers and distributors became responsible for disposing of discarded refrigerators, television sets, air conditioners and washing machines; but the consumer has to pay for their collection.

HENDERSON • Once companies are legally required to recycle, they find they make more money by reclaiming and reconditioning materials. Why didn't they realize this economic advantage before? They didn't because economics failed to give them proper price signals. Subsidies distort prices, and companies are rewarded for using virgin resources. The minute the taxation system is revised to discourage the use of natural resources, necessary changes become possible. Once society passes laws, companies discover that they can make a profit.

IKEDA • We must not leave environmental issues up to market principles. The government and society as a whole must reach consensus and construct a support framework on diverse levels. Can you give an example of a company that profited by recycling?

HENDERSON • Yes, Interface, Inc., the second largest carpet company of its kind in the world. Ray Anderson, president of the firm, decided to sell not carpets per se but a carpeting service. Hotels, airports and so on sign contracts for carpeting, which is laid down in squares. Once a month someone from Interface replaces dirty squares with clean ones. This keeps the carpets looking beautiful all the time. The dirty squares are returned to the factory for reconditioning and reuse. Ray Anderson says that, thanks to this recycling process, his company will be using no virgin materials at all after the year 2005.

IKEDA • A very instructive example.

HENDERSON • We must examine recycling on two levels: the individual and the organizational. Individuals should do all they can and should engage in political work to achieve their goals. In addition, we must force corporations to change their production and marketing methods. We must strongly discourage them from inciting the desire — especially among young people — to buy unnecessary things. Mass-media advertising by commercial companies creates an addiction to material goods all over the world.

IKEDA • To stop it, we need to cultivate what might be called green-minded consumers; that is, people who buy only things that are environment friendly and harmless to the human body.

Along with global warming, the issue of noxious chemical emissions has recently become a matter of great concern. Mothers are anxious about the purity of the atmosphere and the drinking water to which their children are exposed. So-called environmental hormones and substances like dioxin arouse great fear. In Japan, local citizens have often and energetically opposed dioxin-emitting incinerators. What is the situation in the United States?

Attitude goes global

HENDERSON • Many civic organizations in the United States feel we should deal with toxic substances with the kinds of immense lawsuits used against tobacco companies. The United States has a highly effective law called the Toxic Substance Release Register. It requires enterprises to report on chemical substances released from factories and to announce the data publicly.

The attitude it represents is going global. For instance, the United Nations made it part of its protocol.

Though certainly very important, information is not always enough. Sometimes we must resort to legal actions, and we must elect more environmentally responsible politicians. Signatories to the UN Global Compact agree to respect social and environmental standards. But the Compact has no enforcement mechanism or even an auditing system. This situation could end up besmirching the good name of the United Nations itself. This is why my partner, The Calvert Group of socially responsible investment funds, has donated its services to help research the social and environmental performance of the companies that sign the UN Global Compact.

IKEDA • We cannot allow human life and health to take a backseat to the profit motive and arrogant actions of particular companies. At one time, Japan was known as a super-polluter — the Pollution Archipelago. Many people suffered cruelly from pollution-related conditions like the Minamata disease, caused by mercury poisoning, the Niigata Minamata disease, the Itai-Itai disease, and Yokaichi asthma.[2] For years, the government and big business refused to admit responsibility. Even worse, social prejudice and discrimination aggravated the victims' situations.

The writer Michiko Ishimure, who has studied the Minamata sickness issue for years, has said, "In Minamata exists all the aspects of the ordeal of the modern age." The tragedy of environmental pollution does indeed reveal the impasse modern civilization has reached. At the same time, it exposes ugly egoism and profound darkness in the human heart.

Many of the victims were Soka Gakkai members. The meeting I had with some of them in Minamata on January 24, 1974, remains engraved in my mind. I did everything I could to encourage them to struggle with their fate in the hope of altering the destiny of our nation.

Fortunately, after long years of indescribable suffering, some of them bravely regained their health and, as doctors and nurses, now concentrate on research in Minamata-sickness therapy. Others are engaged in large-scale organic farming projects.

The profane path

HENDERSON • Yes, I remember on my first trip to Japan in 1973, I learned about the Minamata tragedy. I met with many environmentalists and also learned of the consumers and farmers cooperating in Seikatsu Clubs, with whom I still keep in touch. Organic farming is so important. As people are learning about the hazard of pesticides, the availability of organically grown produce is now expanding rapidly in the United States and Europe. I can buy all-organic produce at our farmers market in St. Augustine, Florida.

IKEDA • Interest in safe food is increasing in Japan. Homemakers often choose foodstuffs according to how free they are of additives, agricultural chemicals and fertilizer residues. Related to these environmental issues, biotechnology — bioengineering — is now a topic of wide debate in the field of agriculture. Also, we expect much from the field of pharmacology, for instance, in the treatment of hereditary diseases and cancer and with made-to-order medicines.

But we must take into consideration a range of factors, including ecological effects. The utmost caution must be exercised in applying biotechnology to human beings.

We have already heard a lot about cloned sheep and cows. Now scientists are talking about cloning human beings. The idea inspires dread. These topics make big news, as did the completion of the human genome, a kind of human blueprint.

109

HENDERSON • That's very true. In my first book, *Creating Alternative Futures,* I advocated making a deeper understanding of nature and a more sacred view necessary prerequisites of the shift from industrial-machine technology to biotechnology. What eventually happened, however, was that many scientists — tempted by military contracts — pursued a very profane path. Although they did have a deeper understanding of nature, they used it with materialistic intentions instead of with sacred understanding.

In many religious traditions, this sacred understanding of nature is fundamental. In Islamic culture, study of nature is permissible, but intervening and using nature for human purposes are considered profane. Western society lacks this restraint.

IKEDA • Just as other religions find sanctity in human beings and nature, Buddhism, too, teaches that the precious Buddha nature is inherent in all living beings — humans, animals and plants alike. From ancient times, we have instinctively been aware of the irreplaceable value of life. Though people today acquire knowledge at a startling rate, the wisdom to use it properly eludes them. My mentor, Josei Toda, used to say that it's a modern delusion to equate knowledge with wisdom.

The great question, however, is the manner and extent to which we should allow ourselves to intervene in human life and nature. Part of the issue is the way business and science pursue biotechnology without adequate ethical guidelines. At last, in February 2002, the United Nations began drafting a treaty to forbid human cloning.

HENDERSON • Biotechnology is terrifying. I find it absolutely appalling that, without public debate, it has been possible for a baby to be born with the DNA of three parents. It is frightening to have such a development without much public discussion. To investigate things of this kind, I supported the establishment of the Office of Technology Assessment. Until the OTA was finally shut down, it operated under terrible pressure from special interests because it was studying biotechnological issues and the human genome.

But, in an encouraging note, a new book from the Dag Hammarskjöld Institute in Sweden proposes a UN convention on evaluating technological choices. We now need institutions to do on a global scale the kind of work the OTA did.

Global public goods

IKEDA • The possibility of directly manipulating the human genome demonstrates the urgency of correctly handling biotechnology issues. Undeniably, biotechnology can be connected with the discriminatory ideas of eugenics. It must not be left up entirely to government, business and scientists to determine what technologies should be developed and which discoveries should be applied and which abandoned. In addition to the United Nations, people and organizations worldwide must be involved, since biotechnology deals with the lives and deaths of all living beings on the planet. The opinions of all segments of society must be brought into play in drawing up a single model.

HENDERSON • To control biotechnology, we require more global public goods of the kind discussed in a book by that title — *Global Public Goods*, edited by Inge Kaul. In nations, the need for roads, ports, airports, schools and so on is self-evident. On the global level, the book identifies such public goods, which include health, education, environmental protection, justice and peace.

IKEDA • In my peace proposal for the year 2000, I spoke of global public goods in the sense of tangible and intangible social capital transcending boundaries and generations and indispensable to everyone on earth. This is a convincing concept that complements the idea of security for all humanity.

Technology as the hare

HENDERSON • Economists are beginning to realize that they must expand their thinking within a new global framework. For example, Amartya Sen, a Nobel Prize winner in economics, has called peace and justice global public goods.

I compare the technology situation to the fable of the tortoise and the hare. The hare is technology running out of control. The tortoise is society constantly trying to keep up. Because development of technologies for profit is out of control, we need more laws on an international UN level, like the convention on human rights. And we need them now.

IKEDA • The speed with which the technological revolution advances exceeds our imagining. I agree that we need measures within an international framework. Learning from the lesson of nuclear weapons, we must not allow scientific technology to pursue its own path alone.

HENDERSON • Emerging biotechnology is Faustian and arrogant and seems to suggest the end of the human experiment. Many of my American Indian friends have had their DNA sampled only to find out later that some company has patented it. I object to the patenting of life or life forms.

IKEDA • Naturally. It is a travesty against the dignity of life.

HENDERSON • Back in the 1970s, when Jeremy Rifkin was writing *Who Shall Play God?*, we already knew that the U.S.

biotechnology industry was trying to patent life forms. This kind of thing has gone too far. The patents have found their way into the World Trade Organization rules and must be negated. WTO rules on intellectual property are a Western aberration that has led to denial of medicines to the poor and of the right of farmers to use their own seed stocks.

IKEDA • The wisdom to use scientific knowledge properly is necessary. Also, ordinary people themselves must accept responsibility for obtaining and maintaining this wisdom. Absolutely essential to such wisdom is a view of life imbued with compassion and respect for nature and all living things. We must all examine our views of nature and life. Buddhism teaches this wisdom, too.

Each individual human life is related to all other human lives, to life itself and to the cosmic laws. In this time of universal crisis, we must turn our eyes not to our differences but to the things we share in common. We must, as you say, form a coalition based on compassion.

HENDERSON • Yes. In the years to come, recognition of our mutual interdependence will be increasingly important.

EIGHT

The Earth Charter and Environmental Ethics

IKEDA • The World Summit on Sustainable Development took place in Johannesburg, South Africa, August 26–September 4, 2002, a decade after the UN Conference on Environment and Development in Rio de Janeiro, which launched the processes of drafting and ratifying the Earth Charter as a guiding principle for the new environmental century. People have great hopes for this.

A top priority

HENDERSON • I attended the Rio de Janeiro conference as well as the official launch of the Earth Charter in the Peace Palace in The Hague, Netherlands, in 2000. Later I participated in the conference "Earth Dialogues" in Lyon, France, in 2002 and recently became an advisor on the Earth Charter Action Partnership.

The Earth Charter is a top priority for me. This single document contains models for cooperative action on stopping and reversing environmental destruction, preserving and restoring ecological systems, and all the other problems facing the world.

Furthermore it embodies all the shared positive value criteria of humanity today. That is why it must be made known in all corners of the earth.

IKEDA • You have worked for years in the movement to create an Earth Charter.

HENDERSON • The ideas of the Earth Charter were hatched and talked about in Stockholm in 1972, at the UN Conference on the Human Environment. Of course, we lacked the wonderful articulation that has come about over the past twenty-five years. Maurice Strong, secretary-general of the conference, and I were members of a group called the Lindisfarne Fellows, founded by philosopher William Irwin Thompson. That's where I really got to know him and his wife, Hanne. James Lovelock and Lynn Margulis, who developed the Gaia hypothesis that planet earth is one living organism; Amory and Hunter Lovins, Paul Hawken, John and Nancy Todd and other brilliant environmentalists; Richard A. Falk, the legal scholar, and E.F. Schumacher also attended our meetings. We embraced ideas about the wholeness of the human family and the oneness of all phenomena.

IKEDA • With its official declaration on the human environment, the Stockholm conference revealed international society's steps to deal with environmental issues on a global scale. Several other declarations and treaties followed; for instance, the World Charter for Nature of 1982 and the Rio Declaration of 1992. Based on these documents, the Earth Charter strives for a more universal environmental ethic and awareness of humanity. Adoption of the Earth Charter was discussed at the Earth Summit in 1992.

HENDERSON • Yes, and on that occasion — as at the Stockholm conference — I attended as a journalist. Maurice Strong was secretary-general at Rio, too. I remember how disappointed he was that conflict between the industrialized and developing nations prevented the adoption of the Earth Charter. But perhaps it was a good thing that the earlier attempt aborted and allowed the Earth Charter to evolve free of the machinery of nation-states. Actually the failure to adopt it was providential, as it allowed hundreds of grassroots groups all over the world to be involved in the process of shaping and legitimizing the Earth Charter directly.

IKEDA • Later Mr. Strong worked with Mikhail Gorbachev in drafting an Earth Charter. The two co-chaired the Earth Charter Commission, founded in 1995. I understand that Ruud Lubbers, now the UN High Commissioner for Refugees, brought the two men together.

Allies for the earth

HENDERSON • Yes, they are all champions with great conviction and passion. I first met Mr. Gorbachev in Moscow in 1990 at a glittering Kremlin reception for the Parliament of Religious and Spiritual Leaders. Mrs. Gorbachev was there, too. I was thrilled to learn later that both of them were participating in the Earth Charter project.

IKEDA • When I discussed the Earth Charter with Mr. Gorbachev, he said, with an earnest look in his eyes: "Environmental problems are an area in which we must all work together from now on. We should promote the adoption of the Earth Charter in order to protect the world."

Our discussion of environmental education led to mention of his grandchildren. He and his wife, Raisa, seemed very happy. Sadly, she died in 1999. But her achievements in supporting her husband in his efforts to pioneer a new century dedicated to peace and the environment will last forever.

The Rio +5 Forum convened in 1997 to assess the results of the Earth Summit. I believe it also formed the committee that produced the first Earth Charter draft.

HENDERSON • Yes. I was in Rio for that meeting. Steven Rockefeller, chairman of the drafting committee, was there, too, holding endless draft deliberations with many NGOs. It must have been exhausting. I sat in on a series of meetings and listened to everyone voice his or her opinion earnestly. Each subsequent draft was better than the previous one. I am a member of the advisory group formed in 2003 to develop support tools for the Earth Charter Action Partnership, which includes top officials of several cities and organizations.

IKEDA • I have heard how devoted Mr. Rockefeller was to the work. He asked me for comments on the draft. In support of the Earth Charter drafting committee, SGI representatives have widely publicized its work at the grassroots level.

HENDERSON • At the outset, I was unaware of the extent of the support the SGI has given the Charter from its very inception. I once carried a lot of documents to the Boston Research Center for the 21ˢᵗ Century to introduce the Earth Charter. When I got there, to my surprise, I learned that the center staff already had the material. I'm very happy that small incidents like this have brought me closer to the SGI.

IKEDA • By some wonderful chance, the Earth Charter brought us together in friendship.

Boston Center educating public opinion

HENDERSON • Perhaps so. For that reason alone, we must treasure the Charter. The Boston Research Center for the 21st Century has compiled the fruits of its seminars and symposiums on the Earth Charter into documents like *Buddhist Perspectives on the Earth Charter* and *Women's Views on the Earth Charter,* which have done a lot to inform public opinion.

IKEDA • To my delight, the works you mention have received sufficient acclaim so as to be used as teaching materials all over the United States in institutions like Harvard and Columbia. SGI organizations in many countries have held numerous conferences and public-awareness campaigns about the Charter, too.

At last, in June 2000, the long-awaited final version of the Charter was made public at a meeting of the Earth Charter Council in the Peace Palace at The Hague. An SGI member was responsible for the Dutch translation of the Charter text presented to Queen Beatrix.

HENDERSON • The event at The Hague was especially wonderful. The sun streaming through the stained glass windows of the Palace — it was all really magical. I was very excited to have, right before my eyes, an indication of the extremely important role the Earth Charter has to play.

I listened to the many legal scholars who said that the Earth Charter would become internationally recognized as a declaration of human responsibilities to become a counterpart to the Universal Declaration of Human Rights.

IKEDA • On that occasion, Mikhail Gorbachev said that the Earth Charter was more important than any of the fifty significant documents and treaties he signed as president of the Soviet Union. He expressed his pride in this achievement of "our hearts and heads" and called the Charter an expression of the hopes and dreams of millions.

Coming from the man who brought the Cold War to a close, these words carry great weight. What did you feel when you first held the Earth Charter in your hands?

Affirming "people" values

HENDERSON • Intuitively, I knew it was something that needed to be promoted and circulated among all of the world's different communities, though it might take time. Today, the Charter has been endorsed by many cities, hundreds of organizations and some forward-looking companies, including the Calvert Group of socially responsible mutual funds, for which I am an advisor. The Charter touched the deepest level of my being, and I felt drawn to getting involved.

IKEDA • What do you mean exactly?

HENDERSON • From the viewpoint of the oneness of life — essentially, I had tremendous faith that human beings, at their core, wherever they are on this planet and whatever their culture, can come to accept their oneness. I learned that from my mother. Whenever I traveled with her as a kid, no matter the country or language, she always achieved total human-level communication. For her, it was all body language. She would find other mothers, sit with them in parks, admire their babies: "What a lovely baby. May I pick your baby up?"

IKEDA • You evoke a clear image of your mother. The Buddhist scriptures teach us to have the same kind of compassion for all people that a mother demonstrates by being willing to lay down her life for her child. Your mother's compassionate acts were Buddhist teachings in practice. I like to think of SGI mothers being compassionate and encouraging to others as they go about their lives in bright and lively solidarity.

HENDERSON • Because it is imbued with the fundamental viewpoint of life, the Earth Charter is easier for women than for men to accept. It's kind to women — and affirms their values.

IKEDA • In that sense it is in keeping with this Century of Women.

HENDERSON • Quite right. The amazing thing about the Earth Charter process is the careful plodding around among all cultures and patient redrafting and redrafting to include everybody's grassroots ideas.

IKEDA • That is why Maurice Strong called it the peoples' charter. It is truly historic because it really was compiled by the people. The draft was reconsidered over and over again and submitted to many individuals and groups. In this sense, its historic significance may be even greater than that of the Universal Declaration of Human Rights.

The Earth Charter consists of a preamble, sixteen provisions that start with four general principles, and a conclusion. Each provision is further divided into detailed articles. Which elements do you consider most noteworthy?

HENDERSON • The dignified preamble.

IKEDA • It begins: "We stand at a critical moment in Earth's history, a time when humanity must choose its future. . . . The choice is ours: form a global partnership to care for Earth and one another or risk the destruction of ourselves and the diversity of life." But really we have no choice. There is only one way for humanity to survive.

HENDERSON • I agree. To continue: "Fundamental changes are needed in our values, institutions, and ways of living. We must realize that when basic needs have been met, human development is primarily about *being* more, not *having* more."[1]

I consider the idea of being more instead of having more the crux. This is the goal for which we must strive.

IKEDA • Qualitative transformation of contemporary civilization through a revolution of human beings. As Dr. Toynbee once said: "The present threat to mankind's survival can be removed only by a revolutionary change of heart in individual human beings."[2]

HENDERSON • The more we come to grips with our own destinies, expand our awareness, the less acquisitive we become. This is clear from the works of E. F. Schumacher and from Mahatma Gandhi, our great example. Many Christian theologians — among them Meister Eckhart, Martin Buber and Erich Fromm — felt the same way.

IKEDA • The following passage from the preamble deserves our attention: "Humanity is part of a vast evolving universe. Earth, our home, is alive with a unique community of life." This recalls Lovelock's Gaia theory.

You once wrote: "When our human family, at last, see ourselves as a responsible, conscious part of the living body of the Earth, co-creating the future in symbiosis, we will restructure our knowledge, our universities and schools, and our relationships."[3]

Your viewpoint here is very important.

HENDERSON • The book you quoted from was published in 1991 and, even at that early date, included an early version of the Earth Charter. The Earth Charter is a very succinct reflection of the Gaia hypothesis, which has now advanced into more scientific terms as the Gaia theory. It informs a lot of the climate work underlying the Kyoto conference. Indeed, without it as a big pegboard to bring everything together, considerations of vast systems would be impossible.

IKEDA • At the United Nations and in other prominent discussions and debates, a sense of the oneness of all life is gradually becoming an essential philosophical basis for the solution of our global problems.

"All things weave a single whole"

HENDERSON • How does Buddhism interpret the community of life?

IKEDA • Buddhism locates a vast cosmos deep within human life. This cosmos contains a boundless treasure or goodness, reverently called the "Buddha nature." This radiant nature is inherent in all living things. Each inner cosmos is one with the evolving greater external universe. In Buddhist terms, the great universe and the self — the great macrocosm and the microcosm — are one.

Since the self and all phenomena are one, all things are interrelated. Termed *dependent origination*, this teaching explains that all things weave a single whole in which individuals live in relation to all others.

In other words, all beings and phenomena exist or occur because of their relationship with other beings and phenomena, and nothing in either the human or the nonhuman world exists in isolation. All things are mutually related to and interdependent with all other things. They all form a great cosmos maintaining the rhythms of life.

Choosing to guard or to wound

IKEDA • A sense of being part of the great all-inclusive life prompts us to reflect on our own place and on how we ought to live.

Guarding others' lives, the ecology and the earth is the same as protecting one's own life. By like token, wounding them is the same thing as wounding oneself. Consequently, it is the duty of each of us to participate as members of the life community in the evolution of the universe. We can do this by guarding earth's ecological system.

HENDERSON • Your beautiful statement helps me understand why I have so many Buddhist friends! This idea of the one community of life is clearly reflected in the composition of the Earth Charter.

As you said, the text consists of four general principles: I. Respect and Care for the Community of Life; II. Ecological Integrity; III. Social and Economic Justice; and IV. Democracy, Nonviolence, and Peace. The elements of the four principles are all closely interrelated. Under the first of the four are clearly stated four broad commitments.

Starting points for the environment

IKEDA • These commitments, as you call them, provide starting points for dealing with global environmental problems. They are simply expressed as follows:
1. Respect Earth and life in all its diversity.
2. Care for the community of life with understanding, compassion, and love.
3. Build democratic societies that are just, participatory, sustainable, and peaceful.

4. Secure Earth's bounty and beauty for present and future generations.

Articles 5–16 of this section set forth ideas and goals for actually fulfilling these commitments. Which articles do you consider most noteworthy?

HENDERSON • They're all important. But those that reflect the values of women and of indigenous peoples deserve special consideration. Section 11 defines the equality of the sexes and emphasizes extension of women's rights. Section 12 urges consideration of the rights of indigenous populations and minorities. Indeed, the Earth Charter is the first international document of its kind that reflects the values of indigenous people. I know a lot of indigenous people, my friends, who find that in the Earth Charter.

IKEDA • These are important factors ignored by earlier international declarations and documents. Again, to quote from the preamble: "We urgently need a shared vision of basic values to provide an ethical foundation for the emerging world community." The Charter aims to define values common to everyone on earth, including, of course, indigenous peoples. Buddhism makes respect for the dignity of life the foundation of those values. Indeed, without such a foundation, it is hard to create real human solidarity.

Concrete expressions of wisdom

HENDERSON • All of the great religions prominently feature prohibitions against killing, stealing and lying. These models give concrete expression to human wisdom and are important to considerations of global ethics. They are crystallizations of human wisdom.

IKEDA • The pacifist scholar Sissela Bok stresses the importance of constructing earth ethics based on establishing a global minimum standard. Shared traditional religious ethics can be expressed as follows in modern terms.

1. Nonviolence and peace.
2. Fair economics. Prohibition of exploitation.
3. Equality of the sexes and the spirit of communality. This prohibition against sexual exploitation and discrimination relates to racial, ethnic, and cultural equality as well.
4. Trust founded on the ethics of truthfulness. Buddhism goes one step further than forbidding lying by requiring us to speak the truth.

HENDERSON • For five years, I was on President Václav Havel's international advisory board for the Forum 2000 globalization conferences in Prague. A mixture of politicians, spiritual leaders, Nobel Prize winners, poets and famous dissidents attended each of our meetings. Ultimately, we concluded that what Sissela Bok calls "a global ethical minimum that can be identified and worked out cross-culturally" definitely exists.

IKEDA • I still remember the words of advice I asked him to share. He said the important things are to respect each other mutually, to love all humanity as much as we love ourselves, and to live in peace and harmony as sharers of the same planet.

You have studied with the great authority on Buddhist economics, E. F. Schumacher. What are your views on the Earth Charter from the Buddhist standpoint?

Everyone a bodhisattva

HENDERSON • I am not a specialist in religions. But what I really like about the Buddhist tradition is the idea you explained

126

earlier, that everybody possesses the noble bodhisattva life-condition and has boundless potentialities. I am uninterested in priests and liturgies.

I do, however, prize two core religious values. One is the recognition of the supreme light in all life. The other is the golden rule: "Do unto others . . . ." The Earth Charter is an excellent union of these two best aspects of the great religions.

IKEDA • The supreme teachings of Mahayana Buddhism set forth an attitude toward others that is consonant with the golden rule.

"It is like the situation when one faces a mirror and makes a bow of obeisance, the image in the mirror likewise makes a bow of obeisance to oneself."[4]

"If you light a lantern for another, it will also brighten your own way."[5]

These doctrines reveal how actions performed for others from the depths of our beings rebound to our own good. Like the golden rule, they essentially teach us to put ourselves in the other person's shoes.

HENDERSON • That's very important. The spirit of the bodhisattva must be the starting point of all our work in connection with both peace and the environment.

What articles in the Earth Charter do you stress most?

IKEDA • Section 16: Promote a culture of tolerance, nonviolence and peace. Since war is the worst destroyer of the environment, I was especially eager for the Earth Charter to include a pacifist declaration of this kind.

HENDERSON • I, too, agree fully with Section 16. I believe the current U.S. "war on terrorism" should be recast as an international police action with full use of the United Nations, international law and the courts. One thing I like most about the Earth Charter is its mention of our environmental responsibility to the whole life community and to future generations. The preamble mentions a sense of global responsibility; and the final section of the Charter ("The Way Forward") says that to attain the essential renewal of spirit "requires a change of mind and heart. It requires a new sense of global interdependence and universal responsibility."

In this context, *responsibility* is more optimistic than the usual heavier connotation of duty. There's a happiness about it. A happiness in giving that is as great as the happiness of receiving. It's reciprocity, not a burden.

The United Nations — its vital role

IKEDA • In that sense *responsibility* connotes *mission*.

The final section of the Charter refers to support for the United Nations: "In order to build a sustainable global community, the nations of the world must renew their commitment to the United Nations, fulfill their obligations under existing international agreements, and support the implementation of Earth Charter principles with an international legally binding instrument on environment and development."

We have consistently proclaimed the importance of an international order centered on the United Nations and consider the clear statement of the UN role in the Earth Charter profoundly significant.

HENDERSON • I've been a UN supporter for a very long time, and today it is needed more than ever. Of course it needs reforming and updating. The Security Council needs enlarging and to abolish the veto. Still, expression of support for the United Nations in the Earth Charter is very important. I am urging some of my corporate friends who have signed the UN Global Compact to introduce a dialogue between their nine principles of good global corporate citizenship and the sixteen principles of the Earth Charter.

One of the biggest UN problems is the implementation of UN treaties. The organization fosters many treaties that then stagnate and sometimes remain unratified. This is mockingly called "legislative inflation." Everybody I know in international organizations realizes that this is the big issue now. I have opposed current "unilateralist" policies where my country has abrogated many important treaties — even opposing the International Criminal Court. For all action plans — from the Millennium UN Summit to the conferences in Rio, Copenhagen, Vienna, Cairo, Beijing, Johannesburg and so on — implementation is urgent. That was an issue at the March 2002 UN Summit on Financing for Development in Monterrey, Mexico. Many good proposals and resolutions were blocked by the U.S. delegation — including those I and others advocated for taxing currency exchange. This and many other ways of raising funds for the provision of global public goods, health education, clean water, and so on, were blocked by the United States.

IKEDA • The adoption by that summit of what is called the Monterrey Consensus — a new kind of partnership between developed and developing nations directed toward eliminating poverty — is especially significant because of the inseparable nature of development financing and environmental conservation.

HENDERSON • The only way to get fine words, action plans and treaties implemented is grassroots organizing. We need more and more global citizens and NGOs lobbying in their own countries. We still have a lot to do, and popular solidarity is vital.

I spend a lot of time on socially responsible business issues and encouraging voluntary charters such as the UN Global Compact. Some thousand companies have signed the compact, while others have gone further and publicly endorsed the Earth Charter and include it in their managerial policies. So, we're moving things along. In the end, grassroots action propels everything.

IKEDA • I entirely agree. As Maurice Strong says, the Earth Charter will have force only when every individual on this planet masters its meaning. Although they may take time, grassroots movements can alter the current of history. During our global crisis, solidarity among people inwardly compelled to act can provide the driving force for the formation of a truly worldwide set of ethics.

HENDERSON • Yes, and it is important to accompany this evolution of awareness with parallel legal norms. And it must be done quickly. I firmly believe that, if we actually trot the Earth Charter around and organize support chapters in enough places, we can filter out a core endorsable by everybody on the planet. So much more unites us humans than divides us.

Furthermore, I am convinced that the Earth Charter has other big potentialities; for instance, it can become a prototype world constitution for a global communal body. I have introduced the idea to leaders of the World Federalist Association,[6] on whose advisory board I serve, to promote the Earth Charter to their worldwide membership. So far, I have made little progress.

IKEDA • A rereading of the Earth Charter shows the entire document imbued with human wisdom and hope. The twenty-first ought to be a Century of Life and a Century of Women. The Earth Charter is a spiritual mainstay of the effort to make it so.

That is why we must engage and persevere in a grassroots-level public-information campaign to carry the spirit of the Earth Charter to the people. We of the SGI have made a proposal to call the ten years from 2005 the "United Nations decade of education for sustainable development."[7] We must also prepare easy-to-understand, appealing pamphlets presenting the Charter's environmental message to children. Young people are responsible for the future. We must achieve international consensus about devoting energy to youth-oriented environmental education. The Earth Charter is an excellent starting point for such a program.

NINE

The Century of Women

IKEDA • In addition to being a highly discerning futurist, you are an outstanding poet as well. Your candid poems enliven your works on economics and the environment.

I have long been aware of the great strength in the poetry of writers I love, such as Whitman, Hugo and Tagore. They gave me great courage during the struggles of my youth.

Poetry has the power to connect, illuminate and elevate humanity, society and even the cosmos. Unfortunately, today the spirit of poetry is being lost. This is, I feel, one cause of the deepening confusion of our times.

Dear Dorothy—

HENDERSON • I agree entirely. Undeniably science is advancing, and material life is becoming richer. But I seriously doubt we are pioneering new spiritual riches. You are right to say that poetry enriches the spirit and opens our eyes to the true power of humanity.

IKEDA • Among your poems, I especially remember the following one dedicated to your mother.

> *Dear Dorothy — mediating conflicts, instilling ethics*
> *By her actions more than her words.*
> *What fortunate people*
> *We who grew up under her wing!*
> *This is true courage:*
> *To toil each day for others.*
> *This is true valor:*
> *To keep faith with the future,*
> *Without compensation or recognition.*
> *Caring and sharing, honoring Nature*
> *Are de-valued in narrow economics,*
> *While guns, tanks and robots are paraded.*
> *Yet the "love economies" of all the world's Dorothys*
> *Foster life and reign supreme in the cosmic accounts.*[1]

These splendid verses transmit an image of your mother's beautiful, strong and gentle heart. Mothers, of course, play a tremendous role in all our lives. I think some detailed memories of your own mother would be an excellent way to lead into a discussion of one of our main themes, the Century of Women.

HENDERSON • She was a well-educated woman who wanted to be an engineer, and she loved cars. She was one of the first to get a driver's license in her town. Her family was well-to-do. Her mother bought her a car to make up for not letting her become an engineer. She was keenly interested in public affairs and everything that went on in national debates, and she was very well informed. She never got involved in local politics but volunteered for things like Meals-on-Wheels and the Well-Baby Clinic.

IKEDA • Clearly she was very active and well aware of what was happening around her. What are some of the things you learned from her?

HENDERSON • My mother was loving and always had time for us. No matter what happened, if we hurt ourselves or whatever, she always sat down and took us on her knee. She made time for us and was a greatly inspiring role model.

She had no religious tradition. She didn't believe in any god out there. Yet she was the most truly good person I have ever met.

The only thing that really worried me was that she had no authority in the family. My father controlled the finances and everything else. The doubts I entertained about this British patriarchal family — classical for its time — influenced me for the rest of my life.

IKEDA • The same kind of family prevailed in Japan before World War II. As I mentioned earlier, my own father was so old-fashioned that neighbors called him Mr. Hardhead. He was extremely fastidious and tidy. He would run his fingertips over wooden shoji frames and, if he detected dust, would complain about sloppy housekeeping. All the glass in our house was sparkling clean year round. Still, though stubborn and strict, he was a good man who always did his utmost for other people. When I was little, I fell into a pond in the garden. I was screaming and flailing around for dear life. Just as I was about to drown, my father came running and pulled me out. I still vividly remember the strength of his arms as he lifted me from the water.

To honor love

HENDERSON • A stern, but gentle man. Though it is dying out in England today, the patriarchic system is one thing that has prevented women from manifesting their inherent strengths in the home and in society.

As I said, mother was my role model. I wanted to be like her. But she was constantly put down. She couldn't do what she really wanted to, couldn't fully express her gifts because she had no money and no decision-making power in the family.

So I decided that my life would be about reinforcing loving behavior and properly honoring love and loving people. My mother was just like a bodhisattva. She knew that the proper path was to take every opportunity every day to make somebody else's life better. She said we have the power to do it. And that was a powerful lesson for me.

IKEDA • Your mother's way of living and her philosophy of life formed the background against which you advocate what you call the love economy.

HENDERSON • Yes, it did lead me to study the love economy. I kept thinking, "Like my mother, all these people make the world go round and provide all the loving services that hold the community together. They do all the things that enable men to go out and compete in the economic battlefield. Without them, the whole thing would fall apart."

But such lovingly working women do not appear in the economics figures. Their labor is considered worthless. Of course, it's unpaid because it's done out of love with no wish for pay. And this is the kind of thinking that suggested the idea of the love economy.

IKEDA • The peace scholar Johan Galtung, too, remembers how strong an influence his mother exerted on him and stresses the role of women in connection with peace, as in these comments he made in reference to Henrik Ibsen's *A Doll's House:*

"We can clearly imagine what a Nora of our own day would do after leaving Helmer: she would join the peace movement, the environmental movement, the development movement and — above all — the women's movement. In these activities, she would get along better without the Helmer of the play. But instead of abandoning their men as Ibsen's Nora does, today's Noras try to educate them.

"The release of feminine forces long subjugated by the patriarchal system is a boon to a humankind thirsting for peace, a better environment and greater human development."[2]

HENDERSON • The idea of staying at home and educating husbands is important but not sufficient to steer societies toward peace, social justice and ecological balance. As Dr. Galtung implies, mutual respect in the family and the home is a prerequisite for an age of true partnership. Men are good at some things and women at others, but they need not be divided into rigid roles. If the husband is a good cook, he should cook. It is equally as permissible for the wife to run a successful Internet business from the kitchen table in her home, become a scientist, or whatever.

IKEDA • Yes. We should maximize the contributions of both sexes.

HENDERSON • In many instances, when the wife changes her role within the family or goes into business, it affects the husband's self-esteem. But if we address this problem as a function of an evolving economy and act within a truly loving, mutually respectful relation, we will see that a given role should be played by the person best qualified for it. Ideally, we should strive together to create the best framework for the children.

The creative family

IKEDA • I like to think in terms of the creative family. Children remember all their lives mothers who are always optimistic and generous toward society and the community and who live in a creative fashion — as did your mother. That kind of behavior provides the finest possible nourishment for learning how to build a happy home life. It is important for married couples, while giving full rein to their individual characteristics, to cooperate for the happiness of the children, the family and society.

HENDERSON • Such is the current of our times. We initiated civic movements out of concern for our children's future. Most of us who started Citizens for Clean Air were mothers. Since we knew what a big task it is to bring up children, we were anxious that our children have the best future possible. Thinking back, I realize that's what gave us the strength to endure numerous persecutions and keep pushing ahead.

And not just in our group. Women all over the world are pouring love and courage into the family, the neighborhood and into places where economic and governmental policies are being determined. The importance of women to the twenty-first century is incalculable. I think we can restore balance to human society, including the economy, if men and women work together as equal partners.

IKEDA • I agree with you completely. I have always insisted that women must play an important part in the shift from an era of war and violence to an era of peace and harmonious coexistence. Seven hundred years ago, Nichiren spoke out against sexism, saying, "There should be no discrimination among those who propagate the [Lotus Sutra], be they men or women."[3] Like you, I am convinced that, in the twenty-first century, working with men, women can fully manifest their own characteristics and strengths. Indeed, without the cooperative efforts of the sexes, the outlook for humanity is gloomy.

Long experience has taught me that women, by nature, are practical. At the same time, they are compassionate, sensitive and pacifist with a strong sense of justice, seriousness and endurance.

HENDERSON • As world economies evolve toward services and away from goods, heavy industrial activity and muscle power, more and more of the economy will have a female look to it. Women are particularly good in the communications sector and in the love economy, the "caring economy." Many small businesses run by women in community services, mediation, education, daycare and nursing have been set up to meet community needs neglected by government. In the United States, in communities where government has failed, women's businesses have arrived and have figured out how to deliver some of the missing services. These businesses are included in economic statistics and GNP figures, but what is ignored is the equally important amount of volunteerism in the community and the caring for the young and elderly at home. The first estimate of all this unpaid work was made in 1995 by the UN Human Development Report, which explained that $16 trillion was simply missing from global GNP. Eleven trillion dollars was the work of women and $5 trillion of men. If the estimated value of household and family maintenance (in the United States, it is approximated as between $60,000 and $80,000 a year per household) were included in the gross domestic product, this would improve public policy-making and increase respect for the role of homemakers. Volunteerism is gaining recognition as an important contribution to national wealth and well-being.

IKEDA • A very important view. In what specific fields are U.S. women active today?

Morphing into green

Henderson: In all fields. Women have spearheaded the environmental movement, which is now morphing into green businesses. Women run a lot of them and now own or manage almost 50 percent of all private business in the United States. These women are very much leaders in the U.S. economy. Ten million businesses are 50 percent or more women-owned, with 3.9 million of these owned and managed in partnership with men. These companies employ 18.2 million workers and account for $2.3 trillion in revenue.[4]

Women also lead in the area of socially responsible investing — valuing social services like environmental conservation and social welfare. In fact, the U.S. pioneers in the socially responsible investment field were all women: Alice Tepper Marlin, Amy Domini, Susan Davis, Joan Bavaria, Geeta Aiyer, Joanna Underwood, Michaela Walsh and others. Socially responsible investing is now a $2 trillion sector of the economy.[5]

Women are innovators in many ways, such as Rebecca Adamson, founder of First Nations Development Institute; and Leslie Danziger, founder and board chairman of Solaria, the solar energy firm. Partly that is because any group kept out of the main culture tends to think outside the box and come up with innovations to correct things. That sort of group can often see more clearly. Such brilliant "outsiders" include Maude Barlow, national chairperson of the Council of Canadians; Medea Benjamin, founding director of Global Exchange; Ela Bhat, founder of India's Self-Employed Women's Association; and Wangari Mathai of Kenya's Green Belt Movement. Many deserve Nobel economics prizes — which is actually called "The Bank of Sweden Prize in Economic Sciences in Memory of Alfred Nobel." It is not part of Nobel's legacy but set up by the Bank of Sweden to legitimize economics.

IKEDA • Yes, true. What is the background of the impressive emergence of women in the U.S. political arena?

HENDERSON • For a long time women were excluded from U.S. politics, especially at the national level, only gaining the vote in the twentieth century. Big changes are taking place. Women in finance are very conspicuous, often as whistleblowers, for example at Enron. Today, due to tax-cutting, many cities are falling apart. State finances are very bad, and services have been cut. The men who have been mostly in charge have made some of these messes. They abdicate and say, "OK, let the women take over." A woman gets elected mayor or state governor and steps up to the plate to try to clean up the mess — like cleaning up scattered dirty dishes. That's happening in many parts of the United States.

IKEDA • That metaphor is very interesting. Today, the Japanese people are increasingly distrustful of politics. More than ever, we need women with a strong sense of justice and free of any suspicion of corruption to become active politicians. According to the 1999 World Bank report, there is less corruption in nations where there is advanced participation by women.

More than thirty years ago, in 1970, Count Richard Coudenhove-Kalergi, who proposed the idea that grew into the European Union, said to me that when women account for half the membership of every council and every government on earth, we will have laid the strong foundation stone for global peace. I couldn't agree more.

Throughout human history, women have always walked resolutely toward goodness, hope and peace. And women have suffered most when war, violence, oppression, human-rights violations and epidemics have thrown society into turmoil and insecurity. Still they have always risen up in the name of their beloved children and families, determined to build with their own hands a hopeful tomorrow.

With unrivalled tenderness

HENDERSON • This is the true aspect of history but still rarely recognized or documented. Elise Boulding's *The Underside of History* recounted the full story.

IKEDA • I once wrote the following poem in honor of women.

> *Freedom, peace, dignity —*
> *women have been the fighters for these emblems*
> *from times of high antiquity*
> *holding life to be of priceless value*
> *with unrivaled tenderness*
> *taking pains, nourishing,*
> *faithful for a lifetime to these high principles —*
> *these I call true women!* [6]

HENDERSON • A lovely poem. Women are steadily becoming more active in politics throughout the world. I hope that his forecast will come true early in the twenty-first century. Bella Abzug, whom I knew, was the courageous former congresswoman who founded the Women's Environment and Development Organization that promotes gender equity at the United Nations and worldwide.

IKEDA • Which books influenced you as you worked on expanding the important role of women?

HENDERSON • A lot of books opened my eyes to the importance of women's roles following Elise Boulding's books, including books by poet Susan Griffin, by Merlin Stone, Adrienne Rich, Carolyn Merchant, Stephanie Mills, Charlene Spretnak and Riane Eisler.

In the context of human evolution, Mauro Torres, a medical doctor and anthropologist from Colombia, explores the transition from masculine history to the balancing of male and female in his *A Modern Conception of Universal History.*[7]

Up to now, history has been the man's story. Now some wonderful books, including that of Dr. Torres, are saying that at last we are at the beginning of universal history because human societies no longer need to be based on muscle and male hunting power. Brainpower's the thing now, and women have just as much of that as men. This is a scientific basis for the twenty-first to be the Century of Women. It absolutely has to be; the shift must occur. Eventually, we will reach the 50–50 balance at all levels of decision-making between males and females.

IKEDA • The partnership of the sexes — without primacy to one or the other — is the important thing. As is well known, Linus Pauling said that his wise wife's influence inspired him to become a champion of pacifism. Knowing the sorrow of sending a son off to battle, Ava Helen Pauling insisted that we must fight for peace so that war cannot harm our children. Together with her husband, she worked energetically to have nuclear arms abolished. In the era of the McCarthy trials, however, their invaluable work for global peace brought criticism and slander down upon them.

HENDERSON • That was an insane period. Pacifists who had never been communists were branded as Reds and ostracized. Many were blacklisted and couldn't find work. I know how the Paulings must have felt. I, too, was labeled a communist by some, and my family was slandered by others who opposed my environmental work. But I never had to endure any real hardships, and it spurred on my writing and lecturing.

IKEDA • Mr. Pauling spoke of how he was investigated by the authorities and how his passport was confiscated to prevent his going overseas. He lost his position as a university department head. His salary was reduced, and he was forced to give up his laboratory. When I asked how he had remained steadfast throughout all those hard times, he said, "I felt compelled to earn and to keep her (Mrs. Pauling's) respect." Love for his like-minded wife provided maximum support and the driving force for his own activities in the name of world peace.

HENDERSON • That is a moving story. I have always thought that women are behind a lot of men's great deeds, although their work has rarely been documented. Even Milton Friedman, who won the Nobel Prize in economics, actually wrote his books with his wife. Finally, he had to confess it, and now she gets a little bit of the limelight. When I began writing, in the 1960s and '70s, giving men the credit was the conventional way. I knew that Alvin Toffler and his wife, Heidi, were a team. And yet, following the convention of the day, his name went on the books. It's only in the past few years that he — and the cover materials — have been saying that the books are written by both of them. In this age of male–female partnership, joint studies like the ones done by the Friedmans and the Tofflers are going to be all the more valuable.

Generating new values, new roles

IKEDA • That is true. Society must give achievements due recognition, whether they are the work of men or women. Doing so generates new values and energy.

During the twentieth century, many leading women did great things in the name of human dignity and world peace by combating injustice with the mighty spirit of nonviolence. In the United States, Rosa Parks ignited the fire of the civil rights movement. Nadine Gordimer fought against apartheid in South Africa. Rachel Carson, as we discussed, pointed out the gravity of the environmental crisis in *Silent Spring*.

A housewife in New Zealand, horrified by images of the Hiroshima tragedy, became the propelling force behind the World Court Project, which ultimately resulted in an opinion on the illegality of nuclear arms from the International Court of Justice. And a woman, Jody Williams, was the nucleus of the ICBL campaign behind the enactment of the Mine Ban Treaty against the use of antipersonnel land mines.

Which women have influenced you?

HENDERSON • I can't think of any who influenced me during my childhood. As I said, my mother was my role model. Few of the women around me caught my attention. After all, in those days there weren't many woman politicians or business leaders.

But one woman who has always been a role model in the field of peace is Elise Boulding.

Two other women who have deeply influenced me are Barbara Marx Hubbard, the philosopher whom I mentioned previously, and Jean Houston, whose books *The Possible Human* and *The Possible Society* describe the kind of evolution of human consciousness and spirituality that will be necessary for our survival.

Another role model for me was Petra Kelly, who founded the Green Party in Germany. She was first and foremost an environmentalist. Also, she was a great young woman, active in peace, social-justice, and human-rights work. It was very tragic that her life was cut short.

Then, as you say, Rosa Parks in the field of human rights and Rachel Carson in the environmental field. I am very pleased that the SGI has respected Rosa Parks for such a long time.

IKEDA • Rosa Parks's courageous actions, of course, led to the historic bus-boycott movement. Martin Luther King Jr. praised her as a driving force behind the civil rights movement. Mrs. Parks's aims correspond with the goals of the SGI; that is, to inspire the nameless ordinary people to rise up and create a society of universal happiness. Relentless struggle against social injustice and the authoritarian infringement of human rights has been the spirit of the Soka Gakkai since the time of our first president, Makiguchi. It is also the spirit of the SGI.

Women are taking the lead in the SGI peace movement all over the world. In February 2001, as you mentioned, you addressed the "Imagine Peace" conference sponsored by SGI-USA women in Washington, D.C.

HENDERSON • Yes, it was a very significant conference. I supported your naming this the Century of Women and advocated the need for a shift in social values from competition, discrimination, exploitation and waste to cooperation, equality, service and symbiosis.

IKEDA • The theme of the conference was the creation of a culture of peace and women's roles in that effort. One of the speakers was Ivonne A-Baki, the Ecuadorian ambassador to the United States. In an interview conducted during the conference, Ambassador A-Baki was asked how the world would change if all national leaders were women. She replied that, first, there would be no more war because mothers who love their children can scarcely be expected to make and use arms.

She went on to say that too many power-wielders are men. At many of the international problem-solving conferences she had attended, no other women were present. Giving greater prominence to the characteristic female repugnance for arms and violence, she added, would open up new vistas toward resolving international conflicts.

Her words have extra weight because she is the first woman Ecuadorian ambassador and because she has participated in attempts to resolve many conflicts. How do you view her comments?

HENDERSON • I absolutely agree with Ambassador A-Baki. For women, war is nothing but a fearful wastefulness. Women know how much time, love and effort goes into raising a child. When war arises, all that is reduced to nothing and worst of all, the beloved child may be killed. Women find this intolerable. As Ambassador A-Baki says, this is why women's active participation in conflict resolution is of great importance. Take the continuing conflict in the Middle East right now between the Israelis and the Palestinians. I have observed debates between high-level Israeli women and high-level Palestinian women. If those women had been empowered and fully represented in negotiations, there would have been a peace settlement decades ago.

Pay for war, or pay for education

IKEDA • At last, international society is increasingly demanding women's participation in conflict resolutions. In October 2002, the UN Security Council made the epoch-making decision to urge states "to ensure increased representation of women at all decision-making levels in national, regional, and international institutions and mechanisms for the prevention, management, and resolution of conflict."

One positive example of what women can contribute was seen in Burundi. Toward resolving internal conflict in their country, representatives of the All-Party Burundi Women's Peace Conference presented proposals that were reflected in the draft peace accord.

UN Secretary-General Kofi Annan has said that the best strategy for preventing conflict is to expand the role of women as peacemakers. This should become a rule of international society.

In addition to peace, the twenty-first century world requires us to join forces to deal with the issue of education. When I once asked you what you would do if you became president of the United States, you replied that you would make maximum investments in education, which you consider a strategy of primary importance.

HENDERSON • Yes, focusing on children is important for the future. Many agree with me that priorities in the United States are skewed. Almost all politicians say: "Oh yes, education is important"; "We must put more money into education"; "No child left behind"; and so on. And yet, in reality, tax money still short-changes education by subsidizing business corporations and increasing military budgets. It is essential to reform our democracies to get the corruption of money and special interests out of the process.

IKEDA • The same is true in Japan. Such economic and political disregard rebounds hardest on children. Toward breaking out of this situation and reforming education to be a source of happiness to children, I have recently made two proposals: "Serving the Essential Needs of Education" and "Reviving Education."[8]

HENDERSON • I have read your education proposals and agree entirely with the priority you place on children's happiness. We must focus on the kind of education we want for the twenty-first century. How will we fulfill our duty to succeeding generations? Education is important, but we must also give children the love and health care they need. Millions of children in the United States have no health care, no immunization. And yet we're the so-called richest country in the world. What a paradox! This is a shocking indictment of what we really think about children. We do not see them as our future. Of course, education is absolutely vital; but in society as a whole we must revive love and passion for serving our children. Marian Wright Edelman is a leader in this struggle with her Children's Defense Fund.

IKEDA • In many instances in Japan, education concentrates on adjusting the forms — the containers — beautifully and overlooks the all-important children themselves. In my first proposal, I wrote: "Education separated from society can have no vital force; likewise, there is no future for a society that has lost sight of the fact that education is its true mission. Education is not a mere right or obligation. I believe that education in the broadest sense is the mission of every individual. To awaken this awareness throughout society must be the highest priority in all our endeavors."[9] This shows the profound extent to which I agree with what you have said.

HENDERSON • I appreciate your practical contributions in the world to the flourishing of human education. Would you please elaborate on the idea of value-creative education?

"May you always ask yourself this question"

IKEDA • Through institutions like the Soka schools and Soka University, I have devoted all my strength to the flourishing of human education. This is because I believe that education imbued with true humanism is absolutely essential to peace.

Educators themselves, both Tsunesaburo Makiguchi and Josei Toda spent years maturing the idea of Soka University. I made education my primary work in order to realize their ideas.

Soka University opened in 1971, during a period of fiery campus conflicts in Japan. Education had reached an impasse. The times demanded a completely new environment for real learning. Soka University was established in response to that demand. I set the following three ideals for the new institution:

Be the highest seat of learning for humanistic education.
Be the cradle of a new culture.
Be a fortress for the peace of humankind.

Also, the following lines are engraved on one of the pedestals of the pair of bronze statues erected when the university was opened: "For what purpose should one cultivate wisdom? May you always ask yourself this question."

And on the other: "Only labor and devotion to one's mission give life its worth."

These words express my hope that students of Soka University will always think and strive in the name of society, world peace, and the happiness of the masses.

HENDERSON • Lecturing at major universities in the United States, Europe and Asia has taught me that high ideals and clear goals are indispensable to university education. Their clear sense of purpose inspires me to expect much from Soka University and Soka University of America.

IKEDA • Thank you very much. We were happy to inaugurate Soka University of America in Aliso Viejo — in Orange County, California — in May 2001.

We hope that in the years to come you will watch us grow and give us your support. Do you have any advice for Soka University of America?

Teachers and students, one to nine

HENDERSON • Close links between students and teachers such as Soka creates are vital. I think of a young Tamil student from Sri Lanka with whom I am corresponding. I met her in Prague at President Havel's Forum 2000. She courageously spoke of parental abuse in her childhood. I said she could always write to me, and I offered to be kind of a mother figure for her. She has many different skills but doesn't know yet where her highest purpose lies. Of course, this is one of young people's biggest problems.

IKEDA • Yes, and unless they solve it they cannot manifest their strengths. While problems can be the nourishment that helps them grow, unresolved problems can become dead ends where self-confidence and hope are lost.

HENDERSON • Young people need a lot of dialogue with peers and with very loving teachers willing to spend time with them. What they really need is respect. When they get it, they blossom like little flowers.

Confidence is the most important part of education. It opens young people's minds, enabling them to discover their goodness and their own talents. The entire university must strive to produce an environment that instills the confidence with which students can find the right paths and seize the opportunities that come their way. The right atmosphere is almost the opposite of that in places where students are made to focus so hard on technical subjects that they can lose sight of goals.

IKEDA • The whole faculty of Soka University of America is dedicated to giving students the best possible environment. Classes are small to provide plenty of individual attention. A teacher–student ratio of one to nine facilitates plenty of mutual exchange toward refining wisdom and personality.

HENDERSON • I observed all this at Soka. Sincere students and enthusiastic teachers are irreplaceable treasures in university education.

Another ideal of Soka University of America is the cultivation of global citizens who can contribute to creating peace.

The ideal of cultivating pacifist world citizens is needed today more than ever. It helps students to conceive of themselves in a big framework. Once they get the idea that it's OK to dream big dreams, they see that they can make a difference in the world. I have seen this in the positive attitudes of students at Kyung Hee University in Seoul. That's the most important idea to instill, and it's realistic. It's tremendously important. Without such a larger identity, most students underrate themselves and their aspirations.

IKEDA • I am in full agreement with you. I pray that Soka University of America will educate many leaders capable of making contributions to world peace and the happiness of ordinary people. This is the background of the four guidelines I set forth at SUA's founding:

Foster leaders of culture in the community
Foster leaders of humanism in society
Foster leaders of pacifism in the world
Foster leaders for the creative coexistence of nature
and humanity

HENDERSON • The "creative coexistence of nature and humanity" summarizes the environmental curriculum necessary for future generations. It is completely right for peace-related policies to be part of environmental education. I know many environmentalists who just can't handle the idea of conflict resolution and peace. But they must, because war is the worse environmental blight of all. To incorporate peace studies and policies into all aspects of the curriculum is extremely important.

IKEDA • Yes, that fourth guideline derives from the philosophy of Tsunesaburo Makiguchi, who was a great global citizen and environmentalist. The idea that true value is manifest only when human beings live in harmony with nature and society permeated all his books, including his *Geography of Human Life*. I am determined that Soka University of America will train wave after wave of world citizens united in their awareness of global ethics. On foundation day, to conclude my message to the first students, I quoted these lines from Walt Whitman:

Pioneers! O pioneers!

All the past we leave behind,
We debouch upon a newer mightier world, varied world,
Fresh and strong the world we seize, world of labor and
the march . . . .[10]

Education is the source of the pioneering spirit required by humanity in the twenty-first century.

TEN

The Win–Win Society

IKEDA • Let's take up the topic that embodies your vision of the future: the win–win society.

HENDERSON • I like this because it's both one of the goals of our dialogue and a starting point for new action.

IKEDA • You've written that the prevailing system of international politics and global economics sacrifices some nations and peoples. You insist that we must transform that system. I agree with you. You admonish us to realize that, although it may produce temporary winners, law of the jungle competition ultimately makes losers of us all.

Reexamining competition

HENDERSON • Yes, as the environmental situation shows, under current globalization conditions, we must reexamine the old competition rules according to which a few win and all the rest of us lose. If we act solely out of concern for our own interests and comfort, conditions get worse for everybody. If some people in a crowded football stadium insist on standing up to see better, everyone else is eventually forced to stand, too, with the result that no one sees any better and everyone is more uncomfortable. We must realize that this is the kind of world we live in, that building a better society for everybody else has positive results for us, too. And we must live according to this understanding.

IKEDA • A very succinct way to put it. Today, we can clearly see that environmental problems transcend national boundaries.

The German philosopher and educator Josef L. Derbolav once explained that from source to mouth, the Rhine flows through the lands of four peoples. Whether the Rhine is polluted or clean depends on the sense of environmental responsibility of all four.

We are all interrelated environmentally and economically, too. An economic crisis half way round the world affects our own domestic economy instantaneously. As globalization advances, what reforms must we undertake to free our social system from the law of the jungle and create a win–win world?

HENDERSON • We must reexamine our economics indicators and break ourselves of the attachment to putting GNP growth ahead of everything else. For years, the United States and many other countries have set their goals on increasing the GNP. But it is already clear that increased GNP, which ignores social and environmental costs, is no proof of the soundness of a country's economic policies.

The GNP is a material measure. Beyond a certain level, it's like judging adults by a growth index. What we want from adults is not more physical growth but maturity and wisdom.

Qualities of life

IKEDA • In this connection, the Calvert-Henderson Quality of Life Indicators you developed have great significance. They deal with culture, health, education, income, security and peace and order as factors constituting the quality of life.

HENDERSON • Our indicators were developed during the huge GNP and U.S. stock market bubble of the late 1990s. U.S. economists were telling other countries to follow their model because the U.S. economy was the best. And suddenly it all fell apart. The world entered a prolonged recession. The "Washington Consensus" model of economic growth evaporated. Our Calvert-Henderson Indicators, released at the height of the boom, showed clearly that, by our broader measures, the U.S. model wasn't working very well even for the United States. The problems we exposed, in sectors including health, education, human rights, public safety and environment, are today being acknowledged. Our national security indicator warned of the need to restructure our military to address diplomacy, prevention of and information on terrorism — more than a year before the attacks of September 11, 2001. I have presented the Calvert-Henderson indicators in many countries, including the International Conference on Sustainability and Quality of Life Indicators (ICONS), in 2003 in Curitiba, Brazil, attended by seven hundred statisticians from all over the world.[1]

IKEDA • In Japan, too, expanding the GNP was thought to have a bearing on people's happiness. People began calling for reappraisals, however, as soon as the bubble economy burst.

I discussed this matter with John Kenneth Galbraith in 1993. We agreed that it is time to reexamine societies in terms of popular satisfaction and fulfillment. I am convinced that your indicators for evaluating degrees of social happiness are important criteria for the world of the future. The focal point of our time should be moved from the growth of GNP to the inner growth of the human being.

HENDERSON • Other groups have proposed different indices. For instance, as a result of ten years' study, the UN Development Programme devised its Human Development Indices. I worked with Mahbub ul Haq, who originated the concept of human development indices with Inge Kaul, who now heads the UNDP study group. It's too early to say which set of indices works better. I welcome the many new approaches shared at ICONS. The important thing is to have a reflective mirror in which to reexamine society. Human history shows that the United States is only a temporary superpower and imperial overreach has always ended in collapse. With the global war on terrorism and evil and the U.S. economy's lapsing into the red with many problems and weaknesses — huge trade deficits and domestic debt, and dependence on foreign oil — no wonder our dollar fell. The country has many problems and weaknesses. I hope our indicators will stimulate our country to change its ways and step forth on a new, more sustainable path.

On reaching material maturity

IKEDA • Japan faces the same kind of challenge. Problems like the imminent collapse of national financial systems and policies, population aging, falling birthrate and dwindling population cause many to see a dim future. You, on the other hand, think that the Japanese should be more confident and adopt a fresh outlook.

You insist that Japan's troubles are part of a transition from a myopic centering on material economic growth to a more farsighted approach — the long-term building of an economy of sustainable human development. You also think that Japan has a chance to lead the world in the new economy.

HENDERSON • Yes. But to do so, Japan must work hard to make the change of direction firm. I don't know any better way for Japan to turn around than to say, simply: "We have reached material maturity. We're not on the GNP growth model any more. We're on the quality of life model." There is absolutely no reason why they shouldn't make this turnaround. Japan already has better statistics on health, education and infrastructure than has the United States. The Japanese do better on other indicators, too, including the rich–poor income gap, prison conditions and crime rates.

IKEDA • We do have other problems, however, like the graying of the population and a dropping birthrate. Latest analyses predict that the Japanese population will decrease from 2006. Some lament this as national decline. How do you interpret it?

HENDERSON • Viewed in another light, the aging of society and stabilizing population means the gradual maturing of society. Conventional wisdom has it that a slowing of population growth and material consumption is a terrible thing. But I do not agree. An aging society with healthy life-expectancy is maturing and becoming broader so that it can provide leadership for the world in all kinds of ways. Today, older people remain healthy and productive for decades longer than rules allow them to work. Tax and social security laws can be changed to allow them to continue working, paying taxes and contributing to their retirements.

IKEDA • Do you think Japan can call forth its potential strength and create new values to redirect society toward change?

HENDERSON • Yes, absolutely. Japan does have an incredibly good opportunity right now to be a leader in developing new statistics. But it will have to declare its intention to do so, and that will require political will. Because Japan has totally succeeded in the old game of material wealth, why not start the new game of improving the quality of the people's lives?

IKEDA • Indeed some signs of change are already appearing. Because of anxiety about the future, the Japanese today seem to prefer saving to spending. In the past, the economists have said endlessly that the economy depends on consumerism (regarded as a kind of virtue). Some people think this attitude is changing as suggested by decreased spending and increased savings. Clearly, if consumerism continues to dominate the world economy, we will deplete the earth itself.

Japan must cease being concerned exclusively with its own welfare. It must strive to create a happy domestic society while contributing to the welfare of the whole world. Dr. Galbraith is clear that poverty and hunger are especially grave problems and said that he has pondered them deeply throughout his life. He insisted that eliminating poverty is an area where Japan can play a vital role in the twenty-first century.

Roots for the Green Economy

HENDERSON • Yes, Japan can announce to the world that the old game of maximizing material consumption and all-out competition is outmoded and unsustainable. We're no longer going to build entire economies on people's buying more and more stuff they don't need.

Letting an environmentally concerned "Green Economy" take root and opening society outward will take time, but we must realize that there is no other way. Japan can lead in this area, too. The Japanese people can become models for the world by saving more money, for instance, and investing in helping the peoples of Asia and Africa develop solar energy, wind power, hydrogen, clean cars, public transport, health and education. There are many things in which investment provides good returns in completely new areas.

IKEDA • I assume you are talking about the new eco-funds for starting green businesses in developing countries.

HENDERSON • Yes, and domestically as well. Amazingly, none of the new green technologies are getting the amount of investment they need or could use. The European Union has committed matching government funds, but the United States still subsidizes waste, pollution, resource depletion and the dying fossil-fueled industries.

IKEDA • The turnabout necessary in society and the economy requires the complete reconstruction of the field of economics. The Japanese word for economics, *keizai,* is actually an abbreviation of a longer term that means to manage the world and save the people. This indicates another of its goals, at least in theory.

HENDERSON • Very interesting etymology. Economic development is not an end in itself. A harmonious, prosperous society is about human and social development. Economic growth should be a means to that end.

You know my view is that economics is a profession, not a science. A misunderstanding that economics is science causes the trouble. Economics promised more than it could deliver. The Employment Act of 1946 in the United States was the first instance of a country committing itself to full employment by creating a growing economy. Many economists devised the language that went into that act. Of course, it turned out to be very false because they did not have a model of how to implement it. Over the last fifty years, none of their theories and formulas has worked as advertised — creating booms, bubbles and busts, inflation and deflation, unemployment and piling up unrepayable debt. The problem was that the economists' models only tracked the cash transactions — which are only half of the total production. The other half is unpaid work, the importance of which was made invisible to policy-makers. The economists soon began concealing their lack of knowledge by misusing mathematics and statistics to hide their assumptions that economies are in equilibrium and self-regulating by prices and markets. We all see the results of this blindness in today's currency volatility and financial crises.

IKEDA • The economists, then, bear a heavy social responsibility.

HENDERSON • Yes. I have no intention of criticizing all economists. Still, they ought to recognize the influence they exert on society. Economists have made huge mistakes in public policy over the years — for example, the "shock therapy" in Russia and the Argentine collapse to name only two. Their advice has resulted in a tremendous amount of human misery. That's why I proposed in Rio that economists should be certified and held accountable for malpractice, just like doctors. For example, their advice in Russia and the other Eastern European countries was disastrous. China has learned from this and refuses to follow Western economists' advice. Markets are good servants but bad masters.

The starting point is human happiness

IKEDA • Instead of searching for subtle models, economists should start all over from square one, the quest for human happiness. Unlike the natural sciences, economics interprets human beings and prescribes behavior. Traditional economics teaches that human beings follow their desires and work for their satisfaction. Its basic philosophy is optimum distribution of resources to keep all human desires in equilibrium.

HENDERSON • In *Small Is Beautiful,* E. F. Schumacher sharply criticized conventional economics for its vision of humanity. He said that the economics model was completely wrong in defining work as a necessary evil and in claiming that labor is subservient to capital investment and that all human beings maximize their own greed and selfishness. He argued that labor is the unfolding of the meaning of our lives. It's what we do to create or to actualize our potential. The idea that it's some sort of necessary evil that we have to be paid to do is not quite right. Labor has its profoundly cooperative, communitarian and spiritual aspects as well. This is the basis of Bhutan's new Gross National Happiness Index, discussed at ICONS.

IKEDA • Dr. Schumacher looked for answers in Buddhist philosophy and said that, whereas conventional Western economists maximize consumption as a rational structure for production power, Buddhist economics sees consumption as merely a means to human well-being and aims to obtain the maximum of well-being with the minimum of consumption.

HENDERSON • Yes. While claiming that greed, competition, acquisitiveness and selfishness drive the economy, conventional economics pretended to be value-free when actually what the economists projected was a bundle of their own values. This was one of the fundamentals that Fritz Schumacher and I agreed on. Most people in the world have values other than being greedy. They like to share and enjoy giving just as much as receiving. Economists, however, ignored cooperative values and eliminated them from their mathematical models.

Punishing altruism, caring and sharing while rewarding greed, selfishness and competition are a recipe for conflict, poverty gaps and social disintegration.

IKEDA • The sharing and joy in giving you refer to embody true human virtue and the profound and loving attitude of rejoicing in one's own as well as others' happiness. In Buddhism, we call this attitude the bodhisattva way. It is prominent in the humanitarian competition advocated by Tsunesaburo Makiguchi in his *Geography of Human Life*. This book was written in 1903, at a time when nations were striving feverishly for wealth, military might and hegemony. Imperialism and colonialism were rampant throughout the world. Keenly observant of what was going on around him, Mr. Makiguchi categorized the struggle for survival under four headings: military competition, political competition, economic competition and moral/humanitarian competition. He argued that the time had come to deemphasize the first three and concentrate on competition in more humane arenas.

Humanitarian competition — How much can you give away?

HENDERSON • I'd like to hear more about the fascinating idea of humanitarian competition. Is it similar to the indigenous Potlach custom of peoples of the North American West Coast who rank their status by how much they can give away?

IKEDA • It is certainly similar in terms of doing our utmost to serve others. Mr. Makiguchi insisted that we must change not the category — military, political and so on — but the very nature of competition. Ignoring others while striving exclusively for one's own happiness is competition between antagonists. Mr. Makiguchi insisted that we shun this in favor of cooperative competition oriented toward mutual happiness. This is illustrated in the following passage from his book: "It should be understood that 'humanitarian approach' does not imply that there is a specific method which can be designated as such. Rather, it is an effort to plan and conduct whatever strategies, whether political, military or economic, to lead things in a more humanitarian way. The important thing is the setting of a goal of well-being and protection of all people, including oneself but not at the increase of self interest alone. In other words, the aim is the betterment of others and in doing so, one chooses ways that will yield personal benefit as well as benefit to others. It is a conscious effort to create a more harmonious community life."[2]

HENDERSON • This coincides with my own vision of a win–win world. I am impressed that Mr. Makiguchi made the same sort of proposal as long as a century ago.

IKEDA • Sharing and joy in giving play vibrant parts in Buddhist thought, too. For instance, Mahayana Buddhism stresses economics as one aspect of human society and sternly cautions the rich against using their economic gains to monopolize. It teaches that property is a temporary result of causal relationships and is only lent to us.

Buddhism prescribes four ways in which to allot wealth. One quarter must be used to support the family. The second quarter must go to taxes and social welfare. The third should be capital for production. And the fourth should be saved for a rainy day.

The reign of Mauryan King Ashoka around the third century BCE is a classic example of Buddhist economic ethics applied toward creating social and economical prosperity and peace. To expand the economic base, he improved his kingdom's transportation network. In keeping with the principle of universal distribution, he strove to redress economic discrimination. He established a new public office with responsibility for the welfare of women. He incorporated environmental policies and undertook many public projects, like planting roadside trees and providing places for people to rest.

HENDERSON • Wonderful. That kind of economics guides the Ashoka Fellowship founded by William Drayton, which fosters altruistic social entrepreneurs. I am especially impressed by King Ashoka's idea of an office for the welfare of women.

If a king can change his ways

IKEDA • Aggrieved by the folly of his earlier murderous military campaigns, King Ashoka changed his ways and concentrated on policies for the public good. Modern market economics, on the other hand, concentrate on efficiency and rationality and overlook important factors like social justice and human happiness. Humanity still lacks a satisfactory solution to the problem of how to create a sustainable society.

HENDERSON • Fritz Schumacher was completely aware of what you mean in criticizing conventional economics from the environmental standpoint. In *Spaceship Earth,* Barbara Ward pointed to resource distribution as the major problem and to consumption by the rich, not the poor themselves, as the main issue in the population explosion. Kenneth Boulding of the United States and Gunnar Myrdal of Sweden, among other courageous economists in Europe, Latin America and Asia, have made similar statements.

Nonprofit Organizations and NGOs

IKEDA • To create a happy society for oneself and for others, we need a place where people can come together freely and display their individuality and capability; namely, a people's society. In that sense, the role that nonprofit and nongovernmental organizations can play becomes very important. What do you think about this?

HENDERSON • I believe they will play a significant role in the future. The immense NGO third sector is steadily growing and now has a focus in the World Social Forum and via the Internet. A recent example is MoveOn.org, which has opened up a greater public participation in U.S. political processes and elections.

IKEDA • Author and social scientist Peter F. Drucker calls them agencies of human change because they provide places where humans can be transformed into healthier, more cultivated and more dignified beings. The SGI, also an NGO, provides countless people with hope and a chance for a similar revival.

Which nonprofit organizations do you think warrant most attention?

HENDERSON • I am most interested in the ones that promote planetary citizenship and world peace, also those that are trying to create public-access media. There are many such efforts around the world. Today, we live in "media-ocracies" even more than democracies — and these dominant media conglomerates pursue profits by promoting consumerism. So nonprofit organizations and NGOs all need to link together and cooperate to stay in the media rat race. They must work together and barter programming and airtime in the money economy.

For me, the important thing is devising ways to link the nonprofit organizations trying to save the world into a different communication system: a global public-access network linking local communities and NGOs that are moving toward peaceful models of sustainable development. Prototypes can be found on the Internet, radio and television in many countries—

especially Brazil, where the new government of President "Lula" supports wide public participation in shaping Brazil's future.

IKEDA • Civil roles of this kind are already indispensable not only to the economy but also to international policy making. This leads us to talk about the role of civil society — including NGOs — and the United Nations in the twenty-first century.

For years, in my annual peace proposals, I have emphasized the importance of NGOs as people power for a new global society. As an NGO, the Soka Gakkai International is actually supporting many UN undertakings.

You, too, have been actively involved in strengthening the United Nations. What do you think of its role in this century?

HENDERSON • I have long respected your efforts to revitalize the United Nations. We have reached the stage where, without relying on courageous, knowledgeable global citizens, the United Nations cannot fulfill its promise. A proposal I and my partner, Alan Kay, made for funding a standing peacekeeping and humanitarian capability is the UN Security Insurance Agency, now supported by several Nobel prize-winners. Countries that wanted to cut their military budgets could apply for insurance to this agency. The premiums they would pay would fund UN peacekeepers.[3]

For a UN People's Assembly

IKEDA • I first visited the United Nations in October 1960, at the time of the fifteenth sitting of the General Assembly. Cold War tension gripped East and West, and I remember vowing to do what I could to find a solution.

HENDERSON • Really? At that time, I knew almost nothing about the United Nations even though my apartment building was nearby. I had just become a U.S. citizen and was focused on my baby daughter. On cold days, I would walk her in her stroller in the park around the United Nations and browse in the UN bookstore in the visitor's area. I admire you for having worked for the United Nations from such an early time.

IKEDA • The peace, equality and compassion stressed in Buddhist thought are compatible with the course the United Nations pursues. That is why we consider support of the United Nations inevitable.

Half a century has passed since its creation. It is time to strengthen it and make it a driving power for building a global society of peace and harmonious coexistence. I have recommended some reforms, including making the Global Forum — a success at the Rio Summit — a standing organization and proposing a UN People's Assembly of representatives of civil society and a Global People's Council to serve as a UN advisory body.

HENDERSON • It is essential to transform the United Nations into a UN for the people. I am in complete agreement about the importance of the roles of NGOs as people power and the need to set up a UN People's Assembly. I attended meetings of the Global Forum at Rio and agree that it should be made a standing organization. I congratulate you for proposing this. I also agree with making such a Global People's Council a UN advisory body. But the UN People's Assembly, as a secondary UN general assembly, should take precedence over the Global People's Council.

I sometimes call nongovernmental organizations CSOs, or civil-society organizations, because I prefer to use a positive term instead of a negative one beginning with *non*. While *nongovernmental* does not explain the actual status (since corporations are included), the term *civil-society organizations* gives a clearer idea of what they really are: nonprofit, citizen-based and promoting the public interest over special interests.

IKEDA • Very true. I have insisted on the need to regard NGOs as civil or international civil organizations. The term *nongovernmental* overemphasizes the role of the nation-state. Since they act on behalf of humanity and not for any nation-state, NGOs are more suitably described by terms that create a positive image of their responsibility in global society.

Innovation from the periphery

HENDERSON • First, NGOs support social innovation, which always comes from the periphery of any society.

People shut out of current power structures can see problems clearly and come up with innovative ways to cope. For example, as we discussed earlier, Jody Williams's innovation related to the convention to ban antipersonnel land mines could never have been achieved governmentally. The International Criminal Court, too, couldn't have happened without civil-society organizations promoting it. I must add that I am ashamed of President Bush's opposition to the ICC on the flimsiest grounds and his threats to withdraw U.S. troops from UN peacekeeping missions.

IKEDA • Jody Williams redefined the term *superpower* when she said that together we are a superpower if we coordinate our strengths. Certainly not all of our problems related to peace, the environment and human rights can be solved by the existing superpowers or by negotiations among nation-states.

HENDERSON • I agree. Another social innovation that could only have come from civil-society groups is the e-Parliament, started by a young New Zealander named Nick Dunlop. Through the Internet, the e-Parliament will link together all of the parliamentarians in the world who care about the future and sustainability and who support planetary citizenship. Others include the World Social Forum and ISPO, the International Simultaneous Policy Organization, which is a grassroots network in many countries pushing governments to align in policies to reform monetary and financial systems.[4] I support their proposals — based on the work of UK monetary expert James Robertson, a longtime colleague of mine.

IKEDA • None of the mass media is totally free of governmental control. Most are completely one-way — from sender to receiver. The Internet, on the other hand, is interactive. It is more liberal and democratic because it transcends the state to link citizen directly with citizen. The growth of civil society is inseparably linked to media innovation.

Now to return to the United Nations — you established the Global Commission to Fund the United Nations. Grave financial problems, like the U.S. default on its dues payments, can have a serious impact on the future of the United Nations. When Boutros Boutros-Ghali was secretary-general, I suggested broad canvassing of private contributions. In my SGI proposals for 2001, I called for the founding of a UN People's Fund.

HENDERSON • I deeply respect that proposal. We must not allow the United Nations to go on being a hostage to single countries like the United States, which was why I spearheaded the Global Commission and co-edited its report, "The United Nations: Policy and Financing Alternatives" (1995, 1996). There must be other ways. Mitchell Gold, a Canadian activist for world peace education, has been pushing what he calls the One Percent Solution. This involves global credit cards and the paying of 1 percent of every purchase price to a fund for the United

Nations. Some years ago, at one of the Stanley Foundation's meetings on UN financing, and later at a UN conference, I proposed that the United Nations be permitted to sell bonds. If the World Bank can sell bonds, why can't the United Nations? That idea was shot down with a bang. A tax on currency speculation would be another way to finance the United Nations. Citizens groups everywhere think that's a good idea and support various proposals, such as the taxing currency exchange and the FXTRS. According to a U.S. survey Alan Kay and I conducted in the 1990s with the Americans Talk Issues Foundation, 67 percent said yes. Few people approve of currency speculators!

So there's no dearth of good ideas. I don't doubt for a moment that an international tax on financial transactions will someday become a source of funding. It's going to happen, but most governments will resist it every inch of the way.

IKEDA • All of the interesting ideas you mention have vision. The time has come to take concrete action to allow the United Nations to advance from an alliance of nations to the nucleus of a global civil society. To this end, donations from individual nations are important; but so is the broad cultivation of goodwill among the people.

HENDERSON • The United Nations needs to be properly funded, but it also needs more autonomy than it has. It cannot go on being just a trade association of nation-states. It's got to be more than that. This entails reforming and enlarging the Security Council, doing away with the veto, and many other reforms you have proposed, which I fully support. Brazil, which joined the Security Council in 2004, will provide some new leadership.

IKEDA • We have a long way to go to accomplish all the necessary reforms; but the United Nations is the only organization to which we can entrust the future of the peoples of the earth.

Nonetheless, in the present international political climate, when it comes to proposing practical action, many leaders become obsessed with the positions and interests of their own countries and distance themselves from the United Nations.

This is precisely why we must make the citizens of the world aware of the situation and inspire them to arise. As global citizens persevere in expanding their solidarity, we must shift away from international relations centered on narrow or unilateral interests.

A noble spirituality

HENDERSON • I agree. We can create a win–win world when people themselves challenge elites and push for reforms. As you say, solidarity is not enough. Our foundation must be the spiritual awakening of individuals. A truly popular movement goes beyond mere empowerment for personal purposes or advancing one group's agenda, however just. If it stops there, as the histories of socialist revolutions prove, a movement runs the danger of in-group power struggles that lead to corruption and failure. We must avoid this and awaken each person's spirituality. Popular movements lacking in spirituality often do great harm. In contrast, in its work for peace, culture and education, the SGI is founded on human spiritual reformation. That is why I put great hope in the SGI. I, too, am devoting my life to step-by-step progress toward the building of planetary citizenship and a win–win world.

IKEDA • I am convinced that only a movement that awakens the spirituality of each individual and strives to empower the people — one that is by the people and for the people — can become the driving force for true world reformation.

The people's advancement is the foundation on which human society rests. If that foundation is firm, politics and economics will move toward the peaceful, happy horizon of what you call the win–win world.

In a token of gratitude for this dialogue and for the opportunity to work with you toward drawing closer to the solar age of humankind, I conclude with this quotation from the work of Rabindranath Tagore, a poet I have loved since my youth.

> *Today the gates of night's fortress*
> *crumble into the dust —*
> *On the crest of awakening dawn*
> *assurance of new life*
> *proclaims 'Fear Not.'*
> *The great sky responds with paeans*
> *of victory*
> *to the Coming of Man.*

HENDERSON • I am greatly honored and delighted to take part in this dialogue. I offer my heartfelt thanks for the opportunity to share this meaningful discussion. In closing, I offer this poem I wrote recently:

Cyberspace is Sacredspace[5]

> *Earthbound humans*
> *Soaring at last,*
> *In cyberspace.*
> *A leap in their long*
> *And painful journey*
> *Upward: from Olduvai,*
> *Altimira's caves*
> *Catal Huyuk,*
> *Sumer, with waves*

Of patient migration
To cover all the lands
On the bosom
Of Mother Earth.

Cyberspace:
Entrance to the Mind
Of God.
Sacredspace,
Full of promises
Sung by all our sages
From Nomad Gatherer-Hunters
To Agriculture: Gift
Of all our Mothers.
To Industrialization,
Materialism, Consumerism,
Onward to the vaunted
Information Age.

Triumph of Technique
Yet mindlessly playing
Earlier childhood games:
Clicking on trades
In the Global Casino,
Dungeons and dragons.
Escapism from the Sacred Duties
Of Earthbound Life.
More ancient win-lose games,
Netizens crowing
Over Citizens,
Celebrating freedom,
Rights without Responsibilities.

Will we reach
The Age of Knowledge,
Learning at last,
To understand
The mysterious glories
Of Mother Earth
Teeming with Life
Symbiotic with our own?

Will we move on
To the Age of Wisdom
Seeing all Life
As inseparable
On our planetary journey?
Will we use our tools
Of Communication
To reach Community,
And a new Communion
With the Cosmos?
Cyberspace is Sacredspace.

ENDNOTES

CHAPTER 1

1. See Hazel Henderson's "Mr. Bush's Win–Win Option," Interpress Service, Sept. 2001 — www.hazelhenderson.com.
2. Rabindranath Tagore, *English Writings of Tagore* (New Delhi: Sahitya Akademi edition, 1996), p. 41.
3. Arnold Toynbee and Daisaku Ikeda, *Choose Life: A Dialogue* (New York: Oxford University Press, 1989), p. 121.
4. Hazel Henderson, *Paradigms in Progress — Life Beyond Economics* (San Francisco: Berrett-Koehler Publishers, 1995), p. 1; (Japanese edition — Tokyo: Shinhyoron Publishing Co., 1998).
5. Ibid., p. 2.

CHAPTER 2

1. Daisaku Ikeda, *Soka Education* (Santa Monica, Calif.: Middleway Press, 2001), p. 35.
2. In *The Complete Writings of Ralph Waldo Emerson* (New York: William H. Wise, Publisher, 1929). This essay was compiled posthumously, based on a number of Emerson's commencement and other addresses.

CHAPTER 3

1. Norman Cousins and Daisaku Ikeda, *Sekai shimin no taiwa* (Dialogue Between World Citizens), published in 1991.

CHAPTER 4

1. In Hazel Hendson, *Creating Alternative Futures* (West Harford, Conn.: Kumarian Press, 1996), p. viii (in the foreword by Elise Boulding).
2. David Loye, *Darwin's Lost Theory of Love* (Lincoln, Neb.: iUniverse, Inc., 2000).

CHAPTER 6

1. Aurelio Peccei and Daisaku Ikeda, *Before It Is Too Late* (Tokyo: Kodansha International, 1984), p. 152.
2. See Hazel Henderson, "G-8 Economists in Retreat," June 2003, at www.hazelhenderson.com.
3. See Hazel Henderson, "Iraq, the Dollar and the Euro," April 2003, at www.hazelhenderson.com.

CHAPTER 7

1. This system, the FXTRS, is described in Hazel Henderson, *Beyond Globalization* (Bloomfield, Conn.: Kumarian Press, 1999), pp. 44–46.

2. From 1953 to 1958, cases of severe mercury poisoning characterized by neurological degeneration appeared in people who ate fish caught in Japan's Minamata Bay and containing alkyl mercury compounds. Similarly, Itai-Itai disease and Yokaichi asthma are attributed to environmental causes.

CHAPTER 8
1. This phrase was added during one of the Earth Charter consultations at the Boston Research Center for the 21ˢᵗ Century. The Earth Charter is available at www.earthcharter.org.
2. Arnold Toynbee and Daisaku Ikeda, *Choose Life: A Dialogue* (New York: Oxford University Press, 1989), p. 63.
3. Hazel Henderson, *Paradigms in Progress — Life Beyond Economics* (San Francisco: Berrett-Koehler Publishers, 1995), p. 51; (Japanese edition — Tokyo: Shinhyoron Publishing Co., 1998).
4. Nichiko Hori, ed., *Nichiren Daishonin gosho zenshu* (The Collected Works of Nichiren Daishonin) (Tokyo: Soka Gakkai, 1952), p. 769.
5. Ibid., p. 1598.
6. In 2004, the World Federalist Association changed its name to Citizens for Global Solutions.
7. This proposal was accepted at the World Summit on Sustainable Development and approved by the UN General Assembly in December 2002. The UN Decade of Education for Sustainable Development commences in January 2005.

CHAPTER 9
1. Hazel Henderson, *Building a Win–Win World* (San Francisco: Berrett-Koehler Publishers, 1996), pp. ix–x.
2. Johan Galtun and Daisaku Ikeda, *Choose Peace* (London: Pluto Press, 1995), p. 25.
3. Nichiren, *The Writings of Nichiren Daishonin* (Tokyo: Soka Gakkai, 1999), p. 385.
4. From the Center for Women's Business Research News, Washington, D.C., 2003. See www.womensbusinessresearch.org.
5. From www.socialinvest.org.
6. Daisaku Ikeda, *Songs from My Heart* (New York: Weatherhill, 1997), p. 102.
7. See Mauro Torres, *A Modern Conception of Universal History* (Bogota: T/M Editores, 1998).
8. Both proposals can be found in Daisaku Ikeda, *Soka Education* (Santa Monica, Calif.: Middleway Press, 2001).
9. Ibid., p. 95.
10. Walt Whitman, *Leaves of Grass* (New York: W.W. Norton & Company, December 1985).

CHAPTER 10
1. Hazel Henderson, "Statisticians of the World Unite!," Interpress Service, November 2003 at www.hazelhenderson.org.
2. Tsunesaburo Makiguchi, *The Geography of Human Life*, Dayle M. Bethel, ed. (San Francisco: Caddo Gap Press, 2002), p. 286.
3. See Hazel Henderson, *Beyond Globalization* (Bloomfield, Conn.: Kumarian Press, 1999).
4. See www.ispo.org.
5. Published in the Merck Foundation publication *Enough*, 1999.

Index

Index

Index

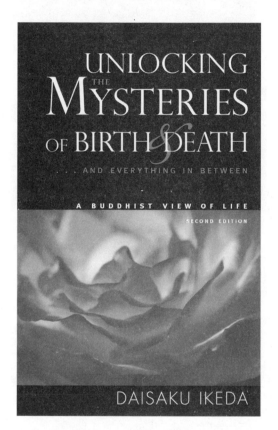

Unlocking the Mysteries of Birth & Death ... and Everything in Between, A Buddhist View of Life (second edition) by Daisaku Ikeda
(ISBN 09723267-0-7; $15.00)

"In this slender volume, Ikeda presents a wealth of profound information in a clear and straightforward style that can be easily absorbed by the interested lay reader. His life's work, and the underlying purpose of this book, is simply to help human beings derive maximum meaning from their lives throught the study of Buddhism."

— FOREWORD MAGAZINE

Choose Hope: Your Role in Waging Peace in the Nuclear Age
by David Krieger and Daisaku Ikeda
Silver Book of the Year Award, 2003, *ForeWord* Magazine
(ISBN 0-9674697-6-7; $23.95)
"In this nuclear age, when the future of humankind is imperiled by irrational strategies, it is imperative to restore sanity to our policies and hope to our destiny. Only a rational analysis of our problems can lead to their solution. This book is an example *par excellence* of a rational approach." — JOSEPH ROTBLAT, NOBEL PEACE PRIZE LAUREATE

For the Sake of Peace: Seven Paths to Global Harmony, A Buddhist Perspective,
by Daisaku Ikeda
Winner of the NAPRA Nautilus Award 2002 for Social Change
(ISBN 0-9674697-9-1; $14.00)
"At a time when we squander enormous amounts of human and environmental resources on the study of and preparation for making war, *For the Sake of Peace* stands as a primary text in the study and practice of making peace."
—NAPRA, Nautilus Award citation

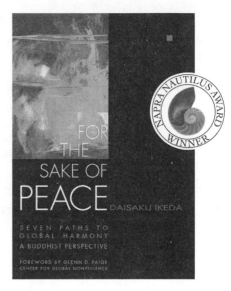

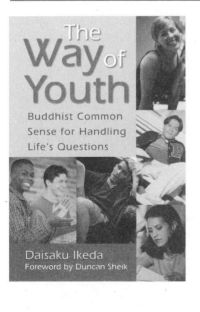

The Way of Youth: Buddhist Common Sense for Handling Life's Questions,
by Daisaku Ikeda
(ISBN 0-9674697-0-8; $14.95)
Also available in Spanish:
A la Manera de los Jovenés
(ISBN 0-9674697-3-2; $14.95)
"[This book] shows the reader how to flourish as a young person in the world today; how to build confidence and character in modern society; learn to live with respect for oneself and others; how to contribute to a positive, free and peaceful society; and find true personal happiness."
—Midwest Book Review

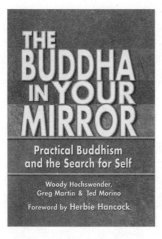

The Buddha in Your Mirror: Practical Buddhism and the Search for Self, by Woody Hochswender, Greg Martin and Ted Morino
(ISBN0-9674697-8-3; $14.00)
Also available in Spanish:
El Buda en tu Espejo
(ISBN 0-9674697-7-5; $14.00)
"Like the Buddha, this book offers practical guidelines to overcome difficulties in everyday life and to be helpful to others. Readers will find these pages are like a helpful and supportive friend. I enthusiastically recommend it."
—Dr. David Chappell, editor of
Buddhist Peacework: Creating Cultures of Peace

Soka Education: A Buddhist Vision for Teachers, Students and Parents, by Daisaku Ikeda
(ISBN 0-9674697-4-0; $23.95)
From the Japanese word meaning "to create value," this book presents a fresh spiritual perspective to question the ultimate purpose of education. Mixing American pragmatism with Buddhist philosophy, the goal of Soka education is the lifelong happiness of the learner.

"[Teachers] will be attracted to Soka and Ikeda's plea that educators bring heart and soul back to education."
—*Teacher* magazine

green
press
INITIATIVE

Printed on recycled paper

Middleway Press is committed to preserving ancient forest and natural resources. We are a member of Green Press Initiative—a nonprofit program dedicated to supporting book publishers in maximizing their use of fiber which is not sourced from ancient or endangered forests. We have elected to print this title on New Leaf EcoBook 100, made with 100% recycled fiber, processed chlorine free. For more information about Green Press Initiative and the use of recycled paper in book publishing, visit www.greenpressinitiative.org.

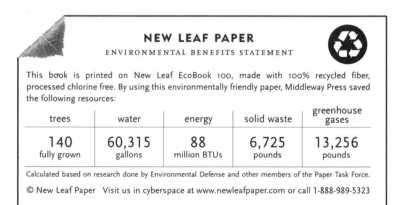

NEW LEAF PAPER
ENVIRONMENTAL BENEFITS STATEMENT

This book is printed on New Leaf EcoBook 100, made with 100% recycled fiber, processed chlorine free. By using this environmentally friendly paper, Middleway Press saved the following resources:

trees	water	energy	solid waste	greenhouse gases
140 fully grown	60,315 gallons	88 million BTUs	6,725 pounds	13,256 pounds

Calculated based on research done by Environmental Defense and other members of the Paper Task Force.

© New Leaf Paper   Visit us in cyberspace at www.newleafpaper.com or call 1-888-989-5323